GUIDE TO THE APPALACHIAN TRAIL
IN PENNSYLVANIA

GUIDE TO

THE APPALACHIAN TRAIL IN PENNSYLVANIA

Number 5 of a Series

SEVENTH EDITION

**Keystone Trails Association
Cogan Station, PA**

1989

Copyright 1989 by
Keystone Trails Association
P.O. Box 251
Cogan Station, PA 17728-0251

All rights reserved. Except in the case of brief quotations embodied in critical articles and reviews, no part of this work may be reproduced or transmitted in any form by any means, electronic or mechanical, including photocopying and recording, or by any information storage or retrieval system, without permission in writing from Keystone Trails Association.

Cover Photo: **POLE STEEPLE SUNSET**
©**Wayne Gross**
ISBN: 0-917953-30-4

CONTENTS

Disclaimer	ix
Preface	xi
Acknowledgments	xii
USING THE GUIDE	**1**
Introduction	1
Abbreviations	2
Metric Conversion Table	3
KEYSTONE TRAILS ASSOCIATION	**4**
THE APPALACHIAN TRAIL	**5**
Trail History	5
The Appalachian Trail Conference	8
THE TRAIL IN PENNSYLVANIA	**9**
Character of the Trail Route	9
History Along the Trail	10
Geology Along the Trail	16
Hawk Mountain Sanctuary	19
LAND OWNERSHIP	**21**
Pennsylvania Game Commission	21
Pennsylvania Bureau of Forestry	22
Pennsylvania Bureau of State Parks	23
Pennsylvania Fish Commission	25
National Park Service	25
Private Land	26

GENERAL INFORMATION 27
- Trail Maintenance 27
- Maintaining Clubs in Pennsylvania 27
- Measurements 28
- Trail Markings 28
- Shelters and Cabins 29
- Maps 30

SUGGESTIONS FOR HIKERS 32
- Fires 32
- Water 32
- Snakes 33
- Dogs 33
- Rabies 34
- Uniform Distress Signal 35
- Transportation 35
- Day Hikes and Short Hikes 36

GENERAL MAP OF A.T IN PENNSYLVANIA 38

SUMMARY OF DISTANCES 40

DETAILED TRAIL DESCRIPTION 43

Section 1: Delaware Water Gap to Wind Gap 43
- North to South 45
- South to North 46

Section 2: Wind Gap to Lehigh Gap 49
- North to South 51
- South to North 53

Section 3: Lehigh Gap to Pa. Route 309 55
  North to South 57
  South to North 59
Section 4: Pa. Route 309 to Port Clinton 61
  North to South 63
  South to North 67
Section 5: Port Clinton to Pa. Route 183 73
  North to South 74
  South to North 77
Section 6: Pa. Route 183 to Swatara Gap 79
  North to South 80
  South to North 83
Section 7: Swatara Gap to Clarks Valley 87
  North to South 89
  South to North 91
Section 8: Clarks Valley to Susquehanna River 95
  North to South 96
  South to North 99
Map of Duncannon 102
Section 9: Susquehanna River to Pa. Route 944 103
  North to South 105
  South to North 107
Section 10: Pa. Route 944 to Churchtown 111
  North to South 113
  South to North 114

Section 11: Churchtown to Pa. Route 94.................... 117
   North to South... 118
   South to North... 120

Section 12: Pa. Route 94 to Pine Grove Furnace 123
   North to South... 124
   South to North... 126

Section 13: Pine Grove Furnace to Caledonia............... 129
   North to South... 131
   Sunset Rocks Trail... 134
   South to North... 135

Section 14: Caledonia to Pen Mar 139
   North to South... 141
   Former Route of A.T.. 144
   South to North... 146

INDEX **149**

DISCLAIMER

Because of constantly changing conditions resulting from natural and other causes beyond the control and/or knowledge of persons and clubs maintaining the Appalachian Trail, Keystone Trails Association and all maintaining clubs and individuals, as well as all authors and contributors to this publication, must disclaim any liability whatsoever for the condition of the trail, occurrences on it, or the accuracy of any data or material set forth in this Trail Guide. This Trail Guide was prepared on the basis of the best knowledge available to the authors at the time of its publication, but readers are encouraged not to place undue reliance upon the continuing validity of the facts set forth herein; and it must be presumed that all persons using the Appalachian Trail and/or this Trail Guide do so at their own risk.

PREFACE

In the Post Office Box of Keystone Trails Association there recently appeared a letter from a 31-year-old architect in Czechoslovakia who asked "if you could send me some information about famous Appalachian Trail." The requested information was provided, of course, but in the process, the letter prompted some reflection on the nature of this Trail that is so much a part of the lives of an ever increasing number of people.

From a flickering dream in the mind of one man, it gradually became first a vision shared by a few, then a commitment on the part of many, and at last a movement supported by a multitude. Now it is an institution known around the world.

In the face of such renown, it is not a little intimidating to be one of a haphazard band of volunteer amateurs presumptuously aspiring to assemble a guidebook for a portion of this national treasure--even if it is only a one-tenth portion. Would it not be better if we all had the grace to withdraw from our various unwanted roles, and leave to credentialed professionals the daunting task of compiling a guidebook?

Perhaps. But then again, perhaps not. What aspect of the Appalachian Trail project has become so ingrained that it is by now virtually inseparable from the Trail itself? Surely nothing is more intrinsic to the Trail than that ragtag army of volunteers who have all along given flesh and blood to the dream. We were there from the beginning, and we are here now-in even greater numbers.

We stumble on the Pennsylvania rocks, even as we slyly boast of them to others. We curse the briers, even as we pick the sun-sweetened berries. We grouse about the commitments that keep us at a desk, and away from the Trail we write about, even as we revel in the words of joy. But through it all we volunteers are the ones who keep aloft the banner of the dream.

So here it is: imperfect, unpolished, and doubtless incomplete, but assembled with affection and served with pride. This seventh edition of the Pennsylvania Appalachian Trail Guidebook is a cooperative production, as detailed in the "Acknowledgements." Many people have been a part of it, and we all hope that you enjoy it as much as we do. Welcome to famous Appalachian Trail.

Maurice J. Forrester, Jr.
Duboistown, PA
December, 1988

ACKNOWLEDGMENTS

A great many people have contributed to the production of this guidebook. To fail to try to acknowledge their help would be gross ingratitude. Still, as has been said before, to list is to omit. It is therefore almost inevitable that in my effort to thank everyone, I shall overlook some. For this I apologize in advance.

First and foremost, thanks must go to the field data collection coordinators who consolidated information for each maintaining club and provided it to me in a usable way. (I must leave it to them to thank all of the many field workers who, in turn, provided them with information.) Listed from north to south according to their Trail maintenance responsibilities, they are:

Springfield Trail Club: Bob Epps
Batona Hiking Club: Mike Seidman
Appalachian Mountain Club: Kent Johnson
Philadelphia Trail Club: John Gall
Allentown Hiking Club: Harold Croxton
Blue Mountain Eagle Climbing Club: George Shollenberger
Brandywine Valley Outing Club: Patrick Markovic
Susquehanna A.T. Club: Craig Dunn
York Hiking Club: Ron Gray
Mountain Club of Maryland: William Schoeneman
Potomac A.T. Club: Ray Fadner and Elizabeth N. Johnston

Much valuable information, assistance, and guidance was also provided by the Appalachian Trail Conference staff, in particular, Bob Proudman, Brian King, Lelia Mellen, and Karen Lutz. Daniel Chazin, an ATC volunteer, who annually edits the **Appalachian Trail Data Book,** also provided many helpful comments. Also working as ATC volunteers were Max and Jean Thomason of Bowling Green, Kentucky, who did a valuable comparative analysis of Trail mileages and other information appearing in various publications.

Our government partners also provided help with this publication. Bill Forrey and Ken Burkholder of the Pennsylvania Bureau of State Parks, Bill Slippey of the Bureau of Forestry, and Roger Lehman of the Game Commission all contributed information. J. Peter Wilshusen of the Pennsylvania Geological Survey submitted the text for the section on geology along the Trail. Material relating to the federal role in the Trail project was provided by Pamela Underhill of the National Park Service.

The section on Hawk Mountain Sanctuary was furnished by the Sanctuary's curator, Jim Brett.

Others who provided information that has contributed to the making of this guide have included (in alphabetical order): Ed Kenna, Paul Robinson, Tom Thwaites, and Dick Tobias. The cover photo is the work of Wayne Gross.

Typesetting and layout was done by Presto Print, and printing and binding by Grit Publishing Company, both of Williamsport, PA.

Finally, I would be remiss not to acknowledge the extensive help contributed by my wife, Mildred, and my son, Kenneth, both of whom helped in a multitude of ways.

— **MJF**

USING THE GUIDE

INTRODUCTION

This Guide is Number Five of a series of guidebooks describing the entire Appalachian Trail from Maine to Georgia. The other books in the series are listed on the back cover.

The book is organized with general and background material at the beginning. Included in this section is information on the history of the Appalachian Trail, the Appalachian Trail Conference, Keystone Trails Association, the nature of the Trail and land ownership in Pennsylvania, and general information for the assistance of hikers.

The bulk of the Guide, making up something more than three-fourths of the total, consists of detailed trail description. The Trail in Pennsylvania is divided into 14 sections of varying lengths. Trail information is given for each section, with general material listed first, followed by detailed description in columnar format, North to South, then South to North.

In preparing this guide book it has been assumed that hikers will supply themselves with the Trail maps published by Keystone Trails Association, based on U.S. Geological Survey maps. For the Trail south of the Susquehanna River, the maps published by the Potomac Appalachian Trail Club may be used in addition to or in place of the KTA maps.

Most automobile road maps, as well as the Pennsylvania Official Transportation Map, show the route of the Appalachian Trail. These can be useful in determining the main highway crossings. A copy of the Official Pennsylvania Map can be obtained without charge by writing to: Pennsylvania Department of Transportation, Harrisburg, PA 17120.

ABBREVIATIONS

ABBREVIATION	MEANING
A.T.	Appalachian Trail
AHC	Allentown Hiking Club
AMC	Appalachian Mountain Club
ATC	Appalachian Trail Conference
BATONA	Batona Hiking Club
BMECC	Blue Mountain Eagle Climbing Club
BVOC	Brandywine Valley Outing Club
ft.	foot/feet
KTA	Keystone Trails Association
MCM	Mountain Club of Maryland
mi.	mile(s)
PATC	Potomac Appalachian Trail Club
PTC	Philadelphia Trail Club
SATC	Susquehanna Appalachian Trail Club
STC	Springfield Trail Club
USGS	U.S. Geological Survey
yd.	yard(s)
YHC	York Hiking Club

MILES TO KILOMETERS CONVERSION TABLE

	0.0	1.0	2.0	3.0	4.0
0.0	0.000	1.609	3.219	4.828	6.437
0.1	0.161	1.770	3.380	4.989	6.598
0.2	0.322	1.931	3.541	5.150	6.759
0.3	0.483	2.092	3.702	5.311	6.920
0.4	0.644	2.253	3.862	5.472	7.081
0.5	0.805	2.414	4.023	5.633	7.242
0.6	0.966	2.575	4.184	5.794	7.403
0.7	1.127	2.736	4.345	5.955	7.564
0.8	1.288	2.897	4.506	6.116	7.725
0.9	1.448	3.058	4.667	6.277	7.886

	5.0	6.0	7.0	8.0	9.0	10.0
0.0	8.047	9.656	11.266	12.875	14.484	16.094
0.1	8.208	9.817	11.426	13.036	14.645	16.254
0.2	8.369	9.978	11.587	13.197	14.806	16.415
0.3	8.530	10.139	11.748	13.358	14.967	16.576
0.4	8.691	10.300	11.909	13.519	15.128	16.737
0.5	8.851	10.461	12.070	13.680	15.289	16.898
0.6	9.012	10.622	12.231	13.840	15.450	17.059
0.7	9.173	10.783	12.392	14.001	15.611	17.220
0.8	9.334	10.944	12.553	14.162	15.772	17.381
0.9	9.495	11.105	12.714	14.323	15.933	17.542

EXAMPLE: to convert 7.4 miles to kilometers.
(1) Find the mile column labeled "7.0".
(2) Find the tenth row for that column labeled "0.4".

The intersection of the mile column and the tenth row will give you the conversion to kilometers, in this case of 11.909 km.

0.01 Miles = .0161 km.

KEYSTONE TRAILS ASSOCIATION

Keystone Trails Association (KTA) is a federation of organizations and individuals sharing a common interest in hiking opportunities in Pennsylvania and neighboring states. Since its founding in 1956 KTA has played a lead role in coordinating the activities of hiking clubs and other sympathetic outdoor groups in and around Pennsylvania. It keeps a watchful eye on actions of government at all levels that can have an impact on hiking or hiking trails. Through the quarterly **NEWSLETTER,** members are kept informed about hiking related activities in Pennsylvania and elsewhere.

One of KTA's major activities is the coordination of management and maintenance efforts relating to the Appalachian Trail in Pennsylvania. This coordination is conducted in close cooperation with the Appalachian Trail Conference, of which KTA is a member. The KTA Appalachian Trail Committee in turn provides the mechanism for coordination among the 11 A.T.-maintaining clubs responsible for Trail segments in Pennsylvania.

In addition to this guidebook and an accompanying map set, KTA also publishes various other books and maps. These include **Pennsylvania Hiking Trails,** a summary guide to more than 2,000 miles of hiking trail in the Keystone State. Also published by KTA are guides to the Tuscarora Trail and the Link Trail, as well as **Geology of the Appalachian Trail in Pennsylvania,** the latter in cooperation with the Pennsylvania Geologic Survey. Write to KTA for a copy of the current price list.

As the pressures of ever expanding development pose growing threats to the integrity of existing trails everywhere, it is important that hikers and their allies band together to guard against attacks, to keep informed, and to present a united front when necessary in the face of incursion. In Pennsylvania, KTA has provided a focus for hiker unity for more than 30 years. New members are always welcome. Dues for individuals are $5.00 per year, and include a subscription to the quarterly **NEWSLETTER.** An annual weekend membership meeting is held every fall, and an open meeting of the governing council is held in the spring.

To join, simply complete and mail the membership application found at the back of this book. If you belong to a group that is interested in affiliating with KTA, have your secretary or another officer get in touch with the KTA President.

KEYSTONE TRAILS ASSOCIATION
P.O. Box 251
Cogan Station, PA 17728-0251

THE APPALACHIAN TRAIL

The Appalachian Trail (A.T.) is a continuous, marked footpath extending along the crest of the Appalachian Mountain range for more than 2,100 miles from Katahdin, a granite monolith in the central Maine wilderness, south to Spring Mountain Georgia.

The Trail traverses 14 states, primarily on public land. Virginia has the longest section with 552 miles, while West Virginia has the shortest, not quite 26 miles along the Virginia/West Virginia boundary, with a short swing into Harpers Ferry near the Maryland border. The highest elevation along the Trail is 6,643 feet at Clingmans Dome in the Great Smoky Mountains. The Trail is only slightly above sea level at its crossing of the Hudson River in New York.

Trail History

Credit for establishing the Trail belongs to three leaders and countless volunteers. The first Trail proposal to appear in print was an article by regional planner Benton MacKaye of Shirley, Massachusetts, entitled, "An Appalachian Trail, a Project in Regional Planning", in the October 1921 issue of the *Journal of the American Institute of Architects*. The author envisioned a footpath along the Appalachian ridgeline where urban people could walk in a natural setting.

MacKaye's challenge kindled considerable interest, but at the time most of the outdoor organizations able to participate in constructing such a trail were east of the Hudson River, where some existing trail systems could be incorporated into the proposed Appalachian Trail. The Appalachian Mountain Club (AMC) maintained an excellent series of trails in New England, but since most ran north and south, the Trail could not cross new Hampshire until the chain of huts built and operated by the AMC permitted an east-west alignment. In Vermont, the southern 100 miles of the Long Trail, then being developed in the Green Mountains, were connected to the White Mountains by the trails of the Dartmouth Outing Club (DOC).

It was in New York during 1923 that in the Harriman-Bear Mountain section of Palisades Interstate Park, the first section of the A.T. was opened by a number of area hiking clubs that had formed the New York-New Jersey Trail Conference.

The Appalachian Trail Conference (ATC) was formed in 1925 to stimulate greater interest in MacKaye's idea and to coordinate the clubs' work in choosing and building the route. The Conference remains a nonprofit educational organization of volunteers dedicated to maintaining, managing, and protecting the Appalachian Trail.

Although interest in the Trail spread to Pennsylvania and New England, little additional work was done until 1926, when Judge Arthur Perkins of Hartford, Connecticut, began persuading groups to locate and cut the footpath through the wilderness. His enthusiasm provided the momentum that carried the Trail idea forward.

In the southern states where there were few trails and fewer clubs, the "skyline" route followed by the A.T. was largely within national forests and parks. Subsequently, a number of clubs were formed in various locations throughout the region to take responsibility for the southern Trail.

Meanwhile, Judge Perkins had interested Myron H. Avery in the Trail. Avery, who chaired the ATC from 1931 to 1952, enlisted the aid and coordinated the work of hundreds of men and women who brought the Trail to its completion on August 14, 1937, when the ridge between Spaulding and Sugerloaf Mountains in Maine became the last section to be opened.

Following the completion of the Trail, the problem of maintaining its wilderness character became increasingly difficult, as highway encroachments, housing developments, and summer resorts caused more and more relocations.

In response to these threats, a plan was proposed by Edward B. Ballard at the eighth general meeting of the Appalachian Trail Conference to establish an "Appalachian Trailway." Under this plan an area on each side of the Trail would be set apart to safeguard the interests of those who travel on foot. Ballard's proposal was accepted by the Conference.

Measures taken to implement this long-range Appalachian Trail protection program culminated first in the execution on October 15, 1938, of an agreement between the National Park Service and the U.S. Forest Service for the promotion of an Appalachian Trailway through the relevant national parks and forests for a distance extending one mile on each side of the Trail. Within this zone, no new parallel roads would be built and no other incompatible development would be allowed. In addition, no timber cutting would be permitted within 200 feet of the Trail. Similar agreements, creating a zone one quarter mile wide, were signed with the states through which the Trail passes.

Three decades of work battling encroachments followed, before Congress, in 1968, established a national system of trails, and designated as the initial components, the Appalachian Trail and the Pacific Crest Trail. The National Trails System Act directs the Secretary of the Interior, in consultation with the Secretary of Agriculture, to administer the Appalachian Trail primarily as a footpath and to protect the Trail against incompatible activities. Provision was also made for acquiring rights-of-way for the Trail both inside and outside the boundaries of federally administered areas.

In 1970, supplemental agreements among the National Park Service, the U.S. Forest Service, and the Appalachian Trail Conference established, under the act, the specific responsibilities of these organizations for the initial mapping, selection of rights-of-way, relocations, maintenance, development, acquisition of land, and protection of a permanent Trail. Agreements also were signed between the Park Service and various states, encouraging each state to acquire and protect a right-of-way for the Trail outside federal land.

The slow progress of federal efforts and the lack of initiative by some states led congress in 1978 to amend the National Trails System Act. The amendment, known as The Appalachian Trail Bill, was signed by President Jimmy Carter on March 21, 1978. The new legislation emphasized the need for Trail protection through the acquisition of a corridor, and authorized $90 million for that purpose. By 1988 fewer than 150 miles remained unprotected, and completion of the project was expected by 1991.

For additional information on the Appalachian Trail, see the following:

Appalachian Trail, by Michael Warren and Sandra Kocker, Portland Graphic Arts Center Publishing Co.. 1979. 104 pp.

The Appalachian Trail, by Ronald M. Fisher, Washington, National Geographic Society, 1972, 199 pp.*

Appalachian Hiker II, by Edward B. Garvey, Oakton, VA, Appalachian Books, 1978, 429 pp.

The Appalachian Trail: Wilderness on the Doorstep, by Ann and Myron Sutton, Philadelphia, J.B. Lippincott, 1967, 180 pp.

Hiking the Appalachian Trail, edited by James R. Hare, Emmaus, PA, Rodale Press, 1978, 2 vols, 2,009 pp.*

The Appalachians, by Maurice Brooks, Riverside Press, 1965, 346 pp.*

Walking With Spring, by Earl V. Shaffer, Harpers Ferry, Appalachian Trail Conference, 1983, 160 pp.

MOUNTAIN ADVENTURE: Exploring the Appalachian Trail, by Ron Fisher, Washington, DC, National Geographic Society, 1988, 199 pp.

---

*Though now out of print, these books are well worth consulting. Try second-hand bookstores or your local public library. If not on your library's shelves, ask about getting them through inter-library loan.

The Appalachian Trail Conference

The Appalachian Trail Conference (ATC) is a volunteer, nonprofit corporation dedicated to the maintenance and preservation of the Appalachian Trail. ATC coordinates the efforts of Trail clubs, state and local governments, the National Park Service, and individuals in Trail Management and maintenance. The Conference publishes booklets of various types and guidebooks for many A.T. sections. Guide books for **all** sections (whether published by ATC or others) are available from the ATC office. In addition, the Conference supplies information on the construction and maintenance of hiking trails and general information on hiking and trail use. The Conference's headquarters is located at Washington and Jackson Streets in Harpers Ferry, WV. Write Appalachian Trail Conference, P.O. Box 807, Harpers Ferry, WV 25425-0807. Phone 304/535-6331. Office hours are 9-5 weekdays and also on weekends from May 15 to October 31.

The membership of the Conference is made up of organizations which maintain the Trail or contribute to the Trail project, individuals who in either personal or official capacity are responsible for the maintenance of secitons of the Trail, and individual dues-paying members.

ATC membership includes a subscription to *Appalachian Trailway News,* published five times a year. The Conference also issues a monthly newsletter, *The Register,* written primarily for Trail maintainers. Guidebooks, maps, and a variety of other publications for hikers and the general public are also published. Membership application material, and complete list of publications, with current prices, are available from the Conference by writing to the address above.

THE TRAIL IN PENNSYLVANIA

Character Of The Trail Route

From the Delaware Water Gap the Trail climbs over 1,100 feet, with views of the river below, before reaching Mt. Minsi. From here the Trail keeps generally to the ridge except for slight dips into Totts Gap and Fox Gap, and (after passing over Wolf's Rocks) a deeper dip into Wind Gap. The whole northern section of the Trail in Pennsylvania is lacking in springs that can be considered reliable after early summer.

After climbing out of Wind Gap, the Trail stays on the ridge, crossing Smith Gap, dipping into and climbing out of Little gap, and then passing over an open rocky area before dropping sharply into Lehigh Gap. Following the climb out of Lehigh Gap, the trail stays on the ridge for nearly 30 miles before dropping down the side and passing near the Hawk Mountain Sanctuary at Eckville. A gradual climb then leads to the Pinnacle, the most spectacular viewpoint along the Trail in Pennsylvania.

The Trail next drops into Windsor Furnace before regaining the ridge, and then dropping steeply to the Schuylkill River. Another 1,000-foot climb leads to 30 more miles of ridgetop hiking until the descent into Swatara Gap. Here the Trail leaves Blue Mountain and traverses St. Anthony's Wilderness, crossing Second Mountain, Sharp Mountain, Stoney Mountain, and finally ascending Peters Mountain which it follows for about 15 miles before dropping steeply to the Susquehanna River.

Beyond the Susquehanna, the Trail turns toward the southwest, crossing Cove Mountain and Blue Mountain before entering the great Cumberland Valley. Here the Trail will be gradually relocated to an off-road route over the coming years thanks to land acquisitions by the National Park Service. At the southern edge of the valley the Trail climbs South Mountain and enters Michaux State Forest, passing through Pine Grove Furnace and Caledonia State Parks before leaving the plateau-like top of the South Mountain range and entering Maryland at Pen Mar.

History Along The Trail

FROM THE DELAWARE RIVER TO THE SUSQUEHANNA RIVER

The Appalachian Trail in this section traverses the crest of Blue Mountain, once known as the Kittatinny Hills and also as North Mountain. The land in general was settled by Germans and a few English, Welsh, and Hollanders, all of whom were fleeing the religious persecution and wars in Europe. Moravians under Count Zinzendorff settled Bethlehem in 1740.

One of the most interesting events, The Walking Purchase, occurred in 1737. Settlers were pushing into this section and crowding the Indians from their lands. After several negotiations with the heirs of William Penn, the Indians agreed to a novel method for deciding territorial limits. The Indians agreed that the proprietors, the Penns, were to receive land measured "as far as a man walks in a day and a half", but this was translated by the white men into "as far as a man **can** walk in a day and a half." Then a line was to be drawn straight to the Delaware River.

Instead of using one man, however, the white men used three; and instead of walking, they almost ran. The distance they managed to cover was 61.25 miles from the starting point near Washington Crossing, PA. Then instead of drawing the boundary line to hit the Delaware River at the nearest point they contrived to come out near the Lackawaxen, thereby doubling the acreage the Indians had expected to grant them.

The Indians accused the proprietors of trickery and dishonesty and The Walking Purchase aroused the bitter hatred of the Delawares. It was this smoldering resentment which was fanned into flames a generation later and broke out in the French and Indian War, creating great havoc in this region. (Read "American Guide Series to Pennsylvania" by the W.P.A. Writers' Program, 1940.)

The Batona Hiking Club of Philadelphia conducts an annual spring endurance hike following the original route of The Walking Purchase from Wrightstown through Pipersville, Harrow, Springtown, Hellertown, Bethlehem, Kridersville, Cherryville, and Lehigh Gap to Mauch Chunk (now Jim Thorpe, PA.)

In the few years prior to the French and Indian War (1754-1763) Indians were attacking so many of the settlements that in 1756 Col. Benjamin Franklin was appointed to build a line of a dozen or more forts and blockhouses from 10 to 15 miles apart to protect the frontier. They paralleled the Appalachian Trail but were down the mountain, somewhat nearer the farms, with an occasional lookout post on the ridge.

From east to west they were as follows: Fort Penn and Dupui's the Fort near Stroudsburg, a blockhouse west of Smith Gap, a blockhouse southwest of Wind Gap, Fort Allen and Fort Lehigh Gap north of Palmerton, Fort Everett at Lynnport, Fort Franklin on the north side of the ridge, Fort Lebanon or Fort Schuylkill near Port Clinton.

Just west of PA Rt. 183, along the Appalachian Trail, is a historical marker for Fort Dietrich Snyder which was the lookout post for Fort Northkill. Next came Fort Henry where there is another marker along the paved road. This was a stockade in half moon shape with a house in the center, provided with a cellar. The walls of the fort were of stone.

Next came Fort Swatara along PA Rt. 72 near Lickdale Furnace and then Fort Manada on the Horse-Shoe Trail. Next, on the banks of the Susquehanna stood Fort Hunter on whose foundations beside U.S. Rt. 22 a museum now stands. No doubt a lookout was usually posted on the high rock above the fort. Fort Harris was a few miles south at the site of Harris's Ferry.

Just off PA 501 near the Trail, is Pilger Ruh (Pilgrim's Rest) Spring, also called Ludwig's Brun. This was used by Conrad Weiser, interpreter and negotiator with the Indians. It was on the route he took between Philadelphia and the Indian capital of Shamokin (now Sunbury).

Count Zinzendorff, Moravian missionary, used this route as early as 1742, as did Chief Shikellimy of the Iroquois Federation. There is a fine statue of Shikellimy in the Conrad Weiser State Park near Womelsdorf, on U.S. 422.

(There are several references to Shikellimy in the "American Guide Series" mentioned above, and a great deal more in Vol. 8 of Pennsylvania German Folklore Society, 1945, entitled "Conrad Weiser, Pennsylvania Peacemaker". A historical novel, "High Wind Rising" by Elsie Singmaster deals with the rise of the Indians against the settlers. Also read "Report of Commission to Locate Frontier Forts of Pennsylvania," 1896.)

St. Anthony's Wilderness

The Appalachian Trail passes through a fine stretch of wilderness, unbroken by habitation for 14 miles between PA Rt. 443 and PA Rt. 325, on land now owned by the Pennsylvania Game Commission.

All through the wilderness are old coal mines which were serviced by a branch of the Reading Railroad over a hundred years ago. The abandoned railroad now serves as a maintenance road for the Game Commission and follows Stony Creek for 15 miles west to Ellendale Forge. Rausch Gap village flourished about 1850, although there is nothing left of it today except a dry stone well about 20 feet from the Trail. The village was populous enough to support a Catholic mission, and there is a small cemetery 150 feet away containing three gravestones of the John Proud family, dated 1853. If other people were buried there, no stones remain to indicate it.

The Appalachian Trail follows an old stage coach road for many miles. Side trails lead down to the railroad stations of Yellow Springs and Cold Springs, near which the Game Commission has planted food plots for the animals and game birds in the valley.

The Jesuits of Philadelphia owned 60 acres at Cold Springs and maintained a summer school for six years. Then in 1880 they sold the property to a syndicate of Harrisburg men who built a summer hotel at a time when mineral baths were very popular. In 1949 there was a YMCA camp at Cold Springs.

On a map printed probably just after the Revolution, based on a 1770 map by W. Scull and made for Thomas and Richard Penn, the area was designated as "St. Anthony's Wilderness". This map also indicated the location of "one of the best gaps in the mountain" slightly to the west of Manada Creek.

Iron industry and Furnaces

All along the Appalachian Trail in Pennsylvania one can see flat round areas, 30 to 50 feet in diameter. These are charcoal hearths where wood was burned into charcoal to fuel the iron furnaces which flourished from 1740 until after the Civil War.

Two miles down from the Trail on the Lehigh Furnace Gap Road are the ruins of the Lehigh Iron Furnace, built in 1826. It is 30 feet high and in fairly good condition.

Also along the Trail, between Eckville and Port Clinton, was the Windsor Furnace, but nothing remains except some glassy slag in the footpath. At one time it was one of the most famous furnaces. Iron stoves were manufactured there and even a replica of The Last Supper in iron.

The furnace at Lickdale has disappeared, but the ruins of Manada Furnace can be found in the bushes along the Horse-Shoe Trail in Manada Gap, nine miles south of the Appalachian Trail. Elizabeth Furnace, once owned by "Baron" Stiegel, is on PA 501. Coleman and Ege were two well known names in the iron industry.

The last furnace before reaching the Susquehanna is Victoria Furnace, 1½ miles down from the Trail on Clarks Creek, near PA Rt. 325. It is in back of Victoria Farms, and is in a good state of repair. Before the Revolution, England insisted that the colonies import her iron products and forbade them from manufacturing their own. Many "bootleg" furnaces were built, hidden away from sight of the main thoroughfares such as the Susquehanna River. Victoria Furnace was such a one.

(A good book to read is "Forges & Furnaces of the Province of Pennsylvania"; Pennsylvania Society of Colonial Dames, 1914.)

SUSQUEHANNA RIVER TO PEN MAR

The following is a condensation of the chapter on History Along the Trail appearing in the "Guide to the Appalachian Trail, Susquehanna River to Shenandoah National Park," published in 1966 by the Potomac Appalachian Trail Club.

Indian Country

The Appalachian Trail crosses the Susquehanna River on the Clarks Ferry Bridge. In 1785 Daniel Clark was operating a ferry here. For the next 13 miles the Trail follows the ridge of Cove Mountain, still a part of the North Mountain range. Then it descends to the Cumberland Valley and again climbs to a ridge on the South Mountain range which is followed all the way to Harpers Ferry, WV.

By the late 1600's this entire region was under the domination of the Iroquois Indians who in 1736 gave title to the west side of the Susquehanna to the Penns. Most of the big wagon trains heading for Ohio passed through Carlisle. (Read Hervey's "Toward the Morning".) In 1704 a licensed Indian trader, Jacques leTort, was settled near Carlisle. Another was George Croghan who settled in Croghans Gap (now Sterretts Gap) in 1741, about two miles from what is now the Appalachian Trail.

Another reminder of the Indian occupation of the South Mountain area is the statue of Mary Jemison, the "White Squaw", which stands near St. Ignatius Catholic Church in Buchanan Valley about five miles northeast of Caledonia Park. As a girl of 15 she was carried off by the Indians, taken to Ohio, and eventually to the Genessee Valley near Letchworth Park in western New York. She became an influential member of the tribe, twice marrying an Indian Chief, and living to the age of 90. In later life she declined an opportunity to return to the society of her childhood.

The Charcoal Iron Industry

The basis of the iron and steel industry was the blast furnace and forge of pre-Revolutionary times. In 1762 there was a furnace, owned by the Ege family, which is still standing at Boiling Springs, and one at Pine Grove where firearms were made for the Revolution. By 1850 there were ten ironworks in the South Mountain area, most on the Cumberland Valley side, but three were near the present Trail.

Pine Grove Furnace

After the Ege family, this furnace was owned by the Watts family. There was a furnace, a forge, coal house, brick mansion house, smith and carpenter shops, 30 log dwellings, grist and saw mills, all drawing on 35,000 acres of land for the necessary charcoal. All along the Trail can be seen the flat charcoal hearths or platforms, 30 to 50 feet in diameter.

All these structures were destroyed by fire in 1915, except the mansion house, the furnace, and the Bunker Hill farm (Rupp House) which is now the Pine Grove Furnace Cabin of the Potomac Appalachian Trail Club, a mile and a half from the furnace. Greenish or bluish bits of the slag can still be found in the Trail.

The railroad that serviced these works in the 1870's followed up Mountain Creek from Laurel Lake. Now it is just a roadbed which is used in part as the Appalachian Trail as it passes Fuller Lake, which was the old ore hole, some 90 feet deep. When the pumps broke down the mine was flooded and abandoned, and soon after 1893 the whole iron works were closed down.

Caledonia Iron Works

The ruins of the furnace which was built in 1837 can be seen in the parking lot at the corner of U.S. Rt. 30 and PA Rt. 233 in Caledonia

State Park. The old blacksmith shop right along the Trail is now a museum. Thaddeus Stevens, the great abolitionist, owned these works at the time of the Civil War. They were destroyed by Confederate troops en route to the Battle of Gettysburg in 1863.

Mt. Alto Iron Works

A few miles west of the Trail in the village of Mt. Alto were the iron works which operated between 1807 and 1893. They consisted of a bloomery (a furnace for making wrought iron), refinery, shops, farms, 20,000 acres of land, and employing 500 persons.

All that remains of the old forge on Little Antietam Creek is the name given to the Old Forge Picnic Grounds bordering the Trail.

Pen Mar Park

(The following is based on "The Western Maryland Railway Story 1852-1952", by Harold A. Williams.)

On the Southern border of Pennsylvania the Appalachian Trail runs through the old Pen Mar Park, built in 1878, which was one of the most famous resorts in the East for more than 60 years. It was owned by the Western Maryland railway, which ran many excursion trains to it to bring clubs, Sunday School picnic groups, etc. on their summer outings. There was an observatory platform at High Rock from which one could see Chambersburg 24 miles away. Included was a fun house, a roller coaster, a miniature railroad, resort hotels and restaurants. Average attendance for such a picnic was 7,000 people, though one Lutheran gathering numbered 15,000.

The Blue Mountain House, half way up to High Rock, built under the auspices of the railroad in 1883, was a great rambling frame building accommodating 400 guests. It was destroyed by a fire in 1913 which was seen many miles away in Waynesboro, PA.

One other large hotel along the Trail was the Buena Vista Springs Hotel where it was said there were more servants than guests. It is now a Catholic school for seminarians, and is adjacent to the golf course.

With the coming of the automobile and a restless generation searching for something new and different, the railroad found that the park was no longer a paying proposition. It was leased by an independent company until 1943 when it was closed and the buildings removed. Gas rationing of World War II put it out of business.

Geology Along The Trail

Introduction. The Appalachian Trail passes through three sections of two physiographic provinces in its 230-mile traverse across the state from the Delaware Water Gap to Pen Mar. These three physiographic regions are:

1. Appalachian Mountain section of the Valley and Ridge province;
2. Great Valley section of the Valley and Ridge province; and
3. South Mountain section of the Blue Ridge province.

Each one of these areas has a characteristic topography which reflects the various rock types present and the geologic history of those rocks. The three sections are described as follows:

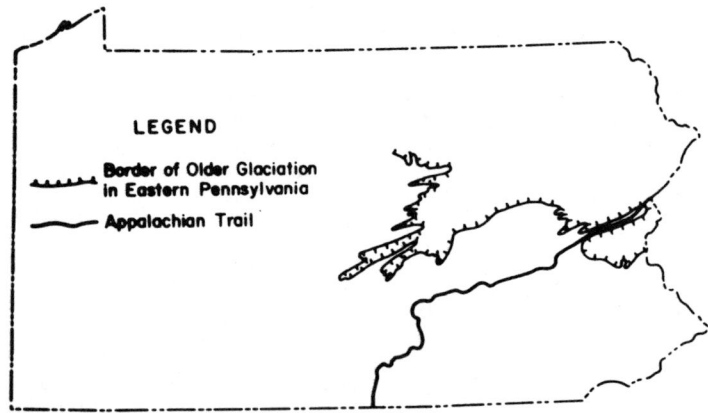

APPALACHIAN MOUNTAIN SECTION:
Valley and Ridge Province

This division extends from the Delaware Water Gap 161.4 miles to PA 944 west of the Susquehanna River and includes Trail Sections 1 through 9. The topography is characterized by long, narrow ridges separated by narrow valleys. The ridges are steep-sided linear mountains with undulating crest lines that are broken periodically by wind gaps and water gaps. These crests are underlain by erosion-resistant quartzites and conglomerates which frequently crop out and are the source of the rock debris often present on the ridge slopes, The ridges sometimes turn back on themselves after long uninterrupted straight stretches in a pattern that reveals the nature of deformed bedrock masses folded into broad anticlines (upfolds) and synclines (downfolds). The mountains rise about 1,000 feet above adjacent valleys which are underlain by more easily eroded shale, siltstone, and limestone.

Bedrock in these mountains ranges in age from 440 to 330 million years; it is sandstone, quartzite, siltstone, conglomerate, shale, and a little coal. Rocks beyond the horizon to the north are younger and those in the valley to the south are older. All of these rock units were deformed by mountain building activity which culminated about 270 million years ago, and changed the original horizontal attitude of the rocks into that of steeply dipping, near vertical, or overturned beds. Millions of years of subsequent erosion has produced the landscape present today.

About 15,000 years ago a continental glacier of thick, scouring ice extended south into Pennsylvania intercepting the area of the Trail in a small section near Delaware Water Gap (map inset). An older continental glaciation, about 150,000 years ago, occupied the valleys on either side of the ridge in Trail Sections 1, 2, and 3, but apparently did not cover the ridge. During these glacial periods, climatic conditions in Pennsylvania beyond the ice border were very severe with intensive freeze-thaw cycles in the higher elevations and probable permafrost in the lower elevations. These conditions subjected the ridge-crest rocks to ice wedging in open fractures. Rock fragments broke away from outcrops and, slid downslope toward the valleys, sometimes covering valley floors with boulder fields, but generally forming boulder accumulations on the mountain flanks. Scattered rock fragments and angular, bedrock outcrops occupy many ridge crests.

GREAT VALLEY SECTION:
Valley and Ridge Province

This division extends from PA 944 at the foot of Blue Mountain 12.4 miles to Yellow Breeches Creek at the foot of South Mountain. It includes Trail Section 10 and part of 11. The topography is characterized by a broad, open undulating valley, part of the Great Valley section extending from central New York through Virginia into Tennessee. The Trail crosses this valley at one of its narrow points (approximately 12 miles) in order to reach South Mountain which merges into the massive Blue Ridge Mountain farther south.

This valley is underlain by intensely deformed limestone, dolomite, and shale with narrow, cross-cutting diabase dikes. The limestone, dolomite, and shale range in age from 560 to 440 million years while the diabase is approximately 180 million years old. All the rock units except the diabase weather readily in the humid Northeast climate. The diabase is more resistant to erosion than the adjacent rocks, standing as a narrow ridge across part of the valley.

SOUTH MOUNTAIN SECTION:
Blue Ridge Province

This division extends from the Yellow Breeches 56.0 miles to Pen Mar and beyond, including Trail Sections 11 through 14. The topography is characterized by rounded, relatively gentle knobs ranging in elevation from about 550 to 1190 feet above the valley floor. White Rocks near the northeastern tip of the province is an exception; there the topography is steep and rugged, capped by a spine of hard, vitreous quartzite bedrock.

The rocks of South Mountain are the oldest encountered along the Trail in Pennsylvania, ranging in age from about 680 to 560 years. These rocks also exhibit the most complex geologic relationships. The mountain range is a broad, composite, anticlinal (upfold) structure that has been thrust along deepseated, regional fault zones during crustal shortening. Bedrock is composed of vitreous quartzite, phyllite, conglomeratic quartzite, graywacke and metamorphosed volcanic rocks, all of which are more resistant to erosion than rocks in adjoining valleys.

The geology of the Appalachian Trail in Pennsylvania is described in greater detail in a publication by the Pennsylvania Geological Survey done in cooperation with the Keystone Trails Association, and available from that organization.

John P. Wilshusen
Pennsylvania Geological Survey

HAWK MOUNTAIN SANCTUARY

The Appalachian Trail passes through a corridor adjacent to the eastern boundary of one of the most famous wildlife areas in the world — Hawk Mountain Sanctuary. The Sanctuary is accessible to A.T. hikers by a blue-blazed side trail which continues along the ridge after the A.T. drops down through the valley to the south or heads north towards PA Rt. 309.

The Sanctuary, founded in 1934, was the first refuge developed to protect birds of prey as they migrated along the ridge in the fall of the year. Prior to its establishment, Hawk Mountain was the gathering place for hundreds of gunners who would engage in the wholesale slaughter of hawks, falcons, and eagles as the birds passed by the North Lookout.

Now persons come from around the world to visit the Sanctuary throughout the year. The greatest influx of visitors comes in the autumn to view the spectacle of the migration. From mid-August through mid-December some 30,000 birds of prey of 14 species can be seen, sometimes at remarkably close range, from one of several lookout points accessible by footpaths.

Early September brings the American Bald Eagle followed by the great Broad-Winged Hawk migration in mid-September. Broad-Wings can be seen in "kettles" of a hundred or more spiraling above the lookouts. October is best for the largest variety of hawks as well as the southward movements of waterfowl. It is also the peak of the autumn coloration. Visitors in late November stand a chance, especially on strong northwest winds, of seeing the Golden Eagle.

The Visitor Center includes exhibits featuring bird of prey ecology and migration, a bookshop, and windows overlooking a feeding station. During fall there are illustrated lectures on Saturday evenings in the Amphitheater.

Since the Sanctuary is a private, non-profit educational institution an admission fee is collected. Hikers are encouraged to use the honor system by making an effort to cover the $2.50 admission charge when they arrive, either by stopping at the Visitor Center entrance gate in the fall, or speaking to a staff member on the North Lookout.

Membership in the Hawk Mountain Sanctuary Association allows free admission to the trails as well as many other benefits. No camping or fires are allowed on Sanctuary property or along the clearly marked Hawk Mountain/A.T. Corridor.

For further information write:

>Hawk Mountain Sanctuary
>Route #2
>Kempton, PA 19529

LAND OWNERSHIP

Pennsylvania Game Commission

The Pennsylvania Game Commission has jurisdiction over more than 1.3 million acres of forest land in Pennsylvania. It receives the major portion of its income from hunting license sales, timber sales, and federal aid reimbursements. The land is managed for the propagation and preservation of wildlife. The Commission is primarily a service agency providing Commonwealth citizens with the opportunity both to hunt and to enjoy wildlife on a non-consumptive basis. The Game Commission recognizes the use of State Game Lands by non-hunters such as photographers, birders, and hikers, and encourages these activities. Financial support of the Game Commission by non-hunters is welcome. Such support can be through the purchase of a license or by participating in programs designed to benefit nongame wildlife. Funds for these programs are raised through sales of wildlife stamps, patches, and prints. Direct contributions can also be made to specific nongame programs such as "Working Together for Wildlife."

The Game Commission has extensive holdings on Blue Mountain, which is the basic route of the Appalachian Trail from west of the Susquehanna River to the Delaware Water Gap. As a result, the major portion of more than 140 miles of Appalachian Trail in this section runs through and is protected by the State Game Lands.

In general, fires and camping are prohibited on State Game Lands. The only exceptions are a few designated areas such as the Rausch Gap Shelter in Game Lands #211. Here, because there is extensive mileage in both directions on the Appalachian Trail within the boundaries of the Game Lands, this shelter was authorized for the use of hikers passing through St. Anthony's Wilderness. Hikers may stay at the shelter for only one night.

The Game Commission **does permit** primitive camping along the Appalachian Trail as it traverses Game Lands. The rules for primitive camping by A.T. hikers in State Game Lands are as follows:
1. Camp within 200 feet of the Trail
2. Camp one night only at any given site.
3. Do **NOT** camp within 500 feet of a water source or public access.
4. **NO** open fires during times of fire hazard.

For more information about Pennsylvania State Game Lands, write:

Pennsylvania Game Commission
2001 Elmerton Avenue
Harrisburg, PA 17110-9797

Pennsylvania Bureau of Forestry

More than 40 miles of the Appalachian Trail in Pennsylvania are located on State Forest lands. About 35 miles are on the Michaux State Forest, which the A.T. crosses shortly after it enters the state from the south, while the remaining five miles are divided between the Weiser and Delaware State Forests.

The purpose of the State Forests, according to law, is: "To provide a continuous supply of timber, lumber, wood and other forest products, to protect the watersheds, conserve the waters, and regulate the flow of rivers and streams of the state, and to furnish opportunities for healthful recreation to the public." State Forest lands are open for the enjoyment of the public by their administrators, the Bureau of Forestry of the Department of Environmental Resources.

The most valuable resource on the Michaux State forest is water. All or part of fifteen municipal watersheds are located on the three Michaux State forest, and collectively they comprise approximately 24% of the total acreage in this forest district. As you walk the Appalachian Trail you will be in or very close to many of these watersheds.

Trail hikers and other visitors to our State Forests are encouraged to look at and become familiar with the types of cutting practices used by the Bureau of Forestry when harvesting timber. Such silvicultural practices make it possible to enhance the quality of various wildlife habitat while producing a continuous supply of wood products.

In addition to the main Trail, there are numerous side trails in the State Forests. These trails generally lead to local points of interest, springs, camping areas, rock outcroppings or scenic overlooks. Camping is permitted along the main Trail and along most of the side trails on State Forest land. Small cooking and warming fires are permitted where adequate precautions are taken to prevent the spread of fire into the forest. All fires are prohibited when the forest fire danger is **high, very high** or **extreme.**

> For more information about State forest land, contact:
> Pennsylvania Department of Environmental Resources
> Bureau of Forestry
> P.O. Box 1467
> Harrisburg, PA 17120

Pennsylvania Bureau of State Parks

There are 114 areas in Pennsylvania administered by the Department of Environmental Resources' Bureau of State Parks. Included in this number are 104 State Parks, three Environmental Education Centers, and six State Parks under design, development or acquisition.

State Parks are dedicated to providing opportunities for wholesome, healthful, satisfying outdoor recreation for all segments of society. The Bureau is committed to protecting, restoring where necessary, and achieving multiple use of the Commonwealth's natural resources. Many parks are located near major urban areas.

Most parks are open year-round, with many facilities available from Memorial Day weekend to Labor Day.

Hiking trails are designated in many parks. Maps and information may be obtained from the appropriate park office. Many parks serve as trailheads for backpacking trails on other public lands. Chief among these is the Appalachian Trail. The A.T. passes through three State Parks. Each one is described below.

Caledonia State Park, 40 Rocky Mountain Road, Fayetteville, PA 17222 (717/352-8419) is one of the oldest State Parks in Pennsylvania. Located in Franklin and Adams Counties midway between Chambersburg and Gettysburg, it is on U.S. Route 30.

Containing 1,130 acres, Caledonia offers many recreational activities. Included are facilities for picnicking, pool swimming, family camping, organized group tenting, an 18-hole golf course, the Totem Pole Summer Playhouse, fishing, hiking, environmental education, and hunting.

The Appalachian Trail passes through the center of the park. Parking for backpackers on extended trips is available. Register at the Park Office.

The history of the park is colorful and varied. The park is named for Thaddeus Stevens's charcoal iron furnace which started operations in 1837. The Honorable Thaddeus Stevens, born in Caledonia County, Vermont, was a famous abolitionist, statesman, and father of the public school system in Pennsylvania.

During the Civil War, the area was visited by Confederate troops who destroyed the furnace in June of 1863.

In 1927, the Pennsylvania Alpine Club reconstructed the stack of the old furnace at a smaller scale. This stack, along with the reconstructed blacksmith shop, is all that remains of the early iron works.

Pine Grove Furnace State Park, R.D. 2, Box 399B, Gardners, PA 17324 (717/486-7174) is located in the heart of Michaux State Forest in southern Cumberland County. The park took its name from the Pine Grove Iron Furnace, the remains of which still stand. The furnace dates back to 1764. Other buildings dating back to the old iron making community also still remain. The historic significance of the area was recognized in 1977 when the iron-making area was entered in the National Register of Historical Places.

The first recreational facilities were built in the area by the railroad. The area was later purchased by the Commonwealth of Pennsylvania in 1913.

Two small lakes are situated within the 696-acre mountain park. The first — Fuller Lake, 1.7 acres in size — was the ore hole from which the iron ore was mined for Pine Grove Furnace. The Fuller Lake recreation area includes facilities for bathing, picnicking, family camping, organized youth group tenting, and fishing.

The second lake is the 25-acre Laurel Lake where picnicking, swimming, nonpower boating, and fishing facilities are available.

The Appalachian Trail passes through the central portion of the park. A parking area near the old iron furnace is provided for the parking of trail hikers' vehicles. Register the vehicle at the park office. A hikers' log is also kept at the park office.

Swatara State Park c/o Memorial Lake State Park, R.D. 1, Box 7045, Grantville, PA (717/865-6470) consists of 3,400 acres extending northward from Swatara Gap for 7.5 miles along the

Swatara Creek Valley. Currently undeveloped, the park nevertheless offers recreational opportunities for hiking, hunting, fishing, trapping, canoeing and rafting, snowmobiling, and ski touring.

Provisions are being made to provide a protected corridor for the Appalachian Trail, which passes through the southwestern portion of the park.

Pennsylvania Fish Commission

At Boiling Springs the Trail will follow a route along the shore of Children's Lake, using a corridor that was acquired by the Trust for Appalachian Trail Lands with the help of a local benefactor and the Pennsylvania Fish Commission. Management of the lake is the responsibility of the Fish Commission.

National Park Service

Pursuant to passage in 1968 of the National Trails System Act, which established the Appalachian Trail as one of the nation's first two National Scenic Trails, the National Park Service (NPS) has undertaken to protect those miles of the Trail that are outside existing state and federal units, and which could not be covered by state protection programs.

NPS's protection program in Pennsylvania is now nearly 85% complete. Eventually nearly 100 miles of the Trail in Pennsylvania will lie in a protected corridor on lands acquired by NPS. In addition to making the necessary connections between existing public lands, the Trail corridor was located to favor the highest land, minimize impacts to private landowners, and take advantage of features attractive to hikers.

In an unprecendented move, the National Park Service in 1984 conveyed to ATC management responsibility for recently acquired NPS lands outside existing federally administered areas. ATC, in turn, has assigned responsibility to its appropriate member clubs. The National Park Service retains a responsibility and an interest in seeing that these lands and their resources are managed "to provide for maximum outdoor recreation potential and for the conservation and enjoyment of the nationally significant scenic, historic, natural or cultural qualities of the areas through which such trails may pass." (Sec. 3b of the National Trails System Act)

The National Park Service remains an active and committed partner in the cooperative management of the Appalachian Trail.

Private Land

Although a very high percentage of the Trail in Pennsylvania is now on publicly owned land, there remain a number of sections that continue to make use of private property. These property owners have every right to expect that their lands will be treated with respect. Failure to do so can lead to needless controversy and difficult problems for Trail managers. As noted above, the hiker should leave no trace of passage. In particular, please note the following:

— Do not destroy trees.
— Do no damage fences or leave gates open.
— Do not litter the Trail.
— Do not disturb crops or animals.
— Be careful of fires; build them only at designated campsites.
— Carry out your trash. If you carried it in, you can carry it out.
— Take nothing but pictures; leave nothing but footprints.

GENERAL INFORMATION

Trail Maintenance

The work of maintaining the shelters and cabins and keeping the trails cleared and blazed is done by volunteers; no one is paid for any Trail work. Each section of the Trail is assigned to some club or individual. You will find the name of the maintaining organization at the beginning of each Trail Description Section under General Information.

Do not attempt to do any Trail marking or relocating on your own. Instead, join a hiking club and offer your services through it. (For a list of the names and addresses of organizations affiliated with Keystone Trails Association, write to KTA, Box 251, Cogan Station, PA 17728.) Hikers should toss aside blowdowns, and clean up around shelters, but if you find any trouble spots that need correcting, please report them to the proper club; or to Keystone Trails Association, P.O. Box 251, Cogan Station, PA 17728; or to the Appalachian Trail Conference, P.O. Box 807, Harpers Ferry, WV 25425.

Maintaining Clubs in Pennsylvania

The Appalachian Trail in Pennsylvania is maintained by the following volunteer clubs, listed from north to south:

Club	Section
Springfield Trail Club	Delaware River to Fox Gap
Batona Hiking Club	Fox Gap to Wind Gap
Delaware Valley Chapter, Appalachian Mountain Club	Wind Gap to Little Gap
Philadelphia Trail Club	Little Gap to Lehigh Furnace Gap Road
Blue Mountain Eagle Climbing Club	Lehigh Furnace Gap Road to Bake Oven Knob Road; Tri-County Corner to Rausch Gap
Allentown Hiking Club	Bake Oven Knob Road to Tri-County Corner
Brandywine Valley Outing Club	Rausch Gap to Pa. Route 325
Susquehanna Appalachian Trail Club	Pa. Route 325 to Pa. Route 225
York Hiking Club	Pa. Route 225 to Susquehanna River
Mountain Club of Maryland	Susquehanna River to Pine Grove Furnace
Potomac Appalachian Trail Club	Pine Grove Furnace to Pen Mar

If you would like to contact any of these clubs directly, write to Keystone Trails Association, Box 251, Cogan Station, PA 17728-0251, for a copy of the latest KTA Directory, which will give you the current address for each of the clubs listed above, as well as much other information about KTA.

Measurements

Distances in this guide book are given in traditional units; e.g., miles, yards, feet. For the benefit of those readers who may be interested, a metric conversion table is printed near the front of this book.

Trail Markings

On some highways the point where the Appalachian Trail crosses is marked by a large brown wood signboard, of which about 100 have been erected by the Pennsylvania Department of Transportation as a public service.

The Trail itself through woods and along roads is marked by white rectangular paint blazes on trees, power or telephone poles, and occasionally on rocks. The standard size for paint blazes is two inches wide by six inches long. Blazes are applied in a vertical position. Also, at intervals the Trail is marked by diamond-shaped metal markers, reading "APPALACHIAN TRAIL — MAINE TO GEORGIA". The paint blazes are at frequent intervals, and hikers should have no difficulty following the Trail if they watch for the blazes.

A "double blaze" (two blazes, one above the other with a space between) is placed as a warning sign. It may indicate an obscure turn or change in direction which might not otherwise be noticed; or it may indicate a change in trail conditions, such as difficult footing.

Important intersections are marked with signs giving distances to nearby roads, other trails, and to shelters or cabins.

A hiker should not go more than a quarter of a mile without seeing a blaze or other Trail indication. If this happens, retrace your steps until you again encounter blazes. Then proceed with caution. Recent timbering operations may have created complications. In such areas use extreme caution. Trail relocations are normally indicated by signs.

Blue blazes indicate a side trail to a spring, viewpoint, shelter, or an access trail.

Yellow blazes are used by State Parks for their boundaries. The yellow blazes of the Horse-Shoe Trail are seen only at its junction with the Appalachian Trail north of Harrisburg. Orange blazes are used for the Tuscarora Trail and the Darlington Trail and other trails. State Forest and State Game Land boundaries are marked with non-uniform white blazes, which can be confusing to hikers. Use caution.

Shelters and Cabins

Open three or four-sided shelters are located along the Trail at varying distances. A spring or other water source is usually nearby.

The shelters were constructed for the benefit of hikers, not for picnickers. All hikers may use them on a "first-come, first-served" basis, and for one night only. They should be shared to the limit of their capacity. Be hospitable, courteous, clean and neat. Leave a clean camp with firewood for the next comer. Burn or take home all refuse and tin cans. If you carry it in, you can carry it out. Be sure your fire is out, even when in a fireplace.

Unfortunately, certain shelters have proven to be highly attractive to vandals. The damage done by these inconsiderate persons, and the condition in which vandalized shelters are sometimes left can render them virtually uninhabitable. Trail maintainers have had to expend an inordinate amount of time, energy and money simply to keep some shelters usable. In some cases shelters have been so extensively damaged that they had to be substantially rebuilt. In some extreme cases shelters have been dismantled and removed. The difficult tasks often encountered in maintaining a shelter have caused problems even in recruiting volunteers willing to accept such an assignment.

All shelter users are encouraged to do whatever they can to encourage respect for these structures and to help reduce the level of vandalism and abuse.

In the division south of the Susquehanna River are four locked cabins managed by the Potomac Appalachian Trail Club. To use these cabins, reservations must be made in advance at PATC's Headquarters, 1718 N Street N.W., Washington, D.C. 20036. Keys will be supplied for definite dates, and a fee is charged for the use of these cabins.

Shelters and cabins are all listed on the pages entitled General Information at the beginning of each section of this guidebook.

Maps

A series of 12 maps showing the route of the Appalachian Trail and connecting side trails throughout Pennsylvania is published by Keystone Trails Association. The maps are specifically designed for use with this guidebook. They can be obtained from KTA (P.O. Box 251, Cogan Station, PA 17728-0251) or from the Appalachian Trail Conference. Write for a current price list.

For the portion of the Pennsylvania A.T. between the Susquehanna River and Pen Mar maps are also published by the Potomac Appalachian Trail Club (P.A.T.C.). These can be used in connection with this guidebook if you prefer. They can be ordered from PATC, 1718 N. St., NW, Washington, DC 20036.

For those desiring more detailed topographic information, the USGS 7½" quadrangle maps are available. They can be purchased from the U.S. Geological Survey, 1200 South Eads St., Arlington, VA 22202. The appropriate quadrangles for the Appalachian Trail are listed below. It is important to note that the A.T. may or may not be shown on these maps, and that when shown, may not be accurate because of the many relocations that have occurred in recent years. It is suggested that if these maps are to be used, the actual route be transferred to them from current KTA maps.

PA. A. T. SECTIONS	USGS QUADRANGLES
Delaware Water Gap to Lehigh Gap	Stroudsburg Saylorsburg Wind Gap Kunkletown Palmerton
Lehigh Gap to Schuylkill Gap	Palmerton Lehighton Slatedale New Tripoli New Ringgold Hamburg Auburn

PA. A. T. SECTIONS	USGS QUADRANGLES
Schuylkill Gap to Swatara Gap	Auburn Friedensburg Swatara Hill Pine Grove Fredericksburg Indiantown Gap
Swatara Gap to Susquehanna River	Indiantown Gap Tower City Grantville Enders Halifax Duncannon
Susquehanna River to Pa. Rt. 94	Duncannon Wertzville Mechanicsburg Dillsburg Mt. Holly Springs
Pa. Rt. 94 to Caledonia	Mt. Holly Springs Dickinson Walnut Bottom Caledonia Park
Caledonia to Pen Mar	Calendonia Park Iron Springs Waynesboro Blue Ridge Summit Smithburg

SUGGESTIONS FOR HIKERS

Fires

The use of small stoves for cooking is recommended in preference to building wood fires, both for safety reasons and to minimize the growing demand for dead wood for such fires. If you do use wood fires for cooking, remember that smaller fires are more efficient than large ones.

Fires are permitted in State Forests at shelters, fireplaces or picnic grounds, except during periods of hire fire danger. Fires should be completely extinguished by pouring water on them. At shelters, leave a supply of food in a sheltered place for the next arrivals.

In State Game Lands, camping and fires are not permitted except at officially authorized sites or as other wise authorized by Game Commission regulations. (See the section on the Pennsylvania Game Commission earlier in this Guide.)

Water

While hiking the A.T. in Pennsylvania, you will encounter water sources such as springs, brooks, and streams at frequent intervals along the Trail. Because the route follows ridge tops for much of its length, however, many water sources tend to dry up during the summer.

All such water sources along the Trail should be assumed to be **CONTAMINATED.**

The mentioning of these sources in this Guide and on the accompanying maps in no way implies their suitability for use. KTA, ATC, and all members clubs and agents expressly disclaim liability for any impurities in such water.

It is best to carry water known to be safe, and to be prepared to use some purification method when using any water source whose purity is in doubt.

It is perhaps useful to mention Giardiasis, an intestinal disorder which occurs with some frequency. It is caused by a microorganism which can be found in untreated "natural" water. The organism, Giardia, is killed at temperatures below boiling. Consequently, boiling water for one minute ensures that the water has been raised to a sufficient temperature to destroy them. This is the preferred treatment. Giardiasis can be temporarily incapacitating, but is not ordinarily life threatening.

Snakes

Snakes may be encountered while hiking the A.T. in Pennsylvania. Contrary to some popular stories, snakes are shy and retiring, and avoid confrontations with humans whenever possible. Two poisonous varieties may be found here: copperheads and timber rattlesnakes. Both species unfortuantely are becoming increasingly rare. If you are careful and quiet, you may be lucky enough to sight one of these inhabitants of Penn's Woods.

The danger from them is small if reasonable care is taken while on the trail. Do not blindly put your hands or feet into openings in rock crevices or ledges. Look carefully before you step into a hidden spot, such as the other side of a log. Move through underbrush with caution.

If given notice, both copperheads\and rattlesnakes will rapidly move out of your way. If you wish to avoid them, you can usually do so by letting them know you are coming. One overseer of an A.T section in Pennsylvania gave the following directions for traversing a rock field on his section of trail where a family of copperheads was known to make its home. Obtain a stick or use your walking stick, if you have one. Tap on the rocks ahead of you as you traverse the rock field. The sounds will set the copperheads scurrying to safety.

In case you are bitten, the safest course is to stop, wait, and send for help, in Pennsylvania help is not too distant from the A.T. Amateur use of snake bite kits can be dangerous and is of dubious value. While very painful, snake bites are rarely fatal, particularly if professional treatment is obtained in a reasonable amount of time.

Dogs

While they may make fine companions for trail hikers, dogs present several problems. When running loose, they often frighten other hikers and wildlife. When the Trail crosses or comes near private land, dogs may trespass on private property to the annoyance of the owner. It is strongly recommended that dogs be leashed when other hikers are nearby and when the trail is on or near private land. In this way your own happy sojourn in the woods will not be at the expense of another hiker's enjoyment, nor will it generate ill will toward the A.T.

Rabies

In recent years the incidence of rabies in Pennsylvania has been increasing, largely in wild animals. Hikers should accordingly be aware both of the existence of the problem and of steps that should be taken if exposure to the disease is suspected.

Rabies is a contagious, potentially fatal disease which is transmitted from one infected animal to another (including humans), primarily through a scratch or bite. Without prompt medical attention, a person who contracts rabies has little chance of surviving. Prudence therefore dictates that you should suspect exposure whenever you experience a bite or scratch from a wild animal or if an animal's saliva comes into contact with a fresh open wound or a break in your skin. Likewise, if the animal's saliva gets in your eye, you can be infected.

If an incident occurs that causes you to fear exposure, make every effort to secure the suspected animal. This may not be easy to do, but the only way to determine if you have in fact been exposed is to have the animal's brain examined by qualified laboratory personnel. Consequently, in securing the animal an effort should be made to avoid damaging the brain.

Whether or not you are able to secure the suspected animal, you should get yourself promptly to a doctor or hospital for treatment and further guidance. If the animal has been secured and tests subsequently show that it was not rabid, you should have no more problems than you would from any cut or scratch. On the other hand, if the animal is found to have rabies, then you will have to undergo treatment to prevent the development of the disease in your own system.

If the offending animal has not been captured or killed, it is likely that your doctor will recommend these treatments as a precautionary measure. Herein lies the importance of having the animal available for testing; this can avoid the inconvenience and discomfort of unnecessary treatment.

The Pennsylvania Department of Health has a 24-hour telephone number (215) 363-8500 that you can call for advice or for further instructions, if necessary.

Uniform Distress Signals

Hikers who find themselves in difficulty while on the trail should utilize the standard method for seeking help. This consists of three short calls--audible or visible--repeated at regular intervals. In daylight a whistle or other audible call, a light flashed with a mirror, or smoke puffs made with a coat and smudge fire may be used. At night a flashlight or three small, bright fires can be substituted.

Such a signal is for emergency use only. Anyone recognizing the signal is honor bound to set about making the rescue at once or to summon more competent aid, since delay may mean disaster. Likewise, the distressed party has an obligation to recompense the rescuers for their time and trouble in extending aid.

Anyone receiving a distress signal should acknowledge it by a signal of two calls, if possible by the same method as that used in the distress call. Whenever practical, local or state police should be notified to avoid duplication of rescue parties.

It is recommended that when hiking, a whistle be routinely carried for use in such emergencies.

Transportation

Public transportation to the Appalachian Trail is essentially limited to bus transportation, and then only to a few trailheads. Following is a list of points on the Pennsylvania A.T where, at last report, scheduled bus service was still available. Because of the frequently changing nature of bus schedules, however, this information is subject to confirmation at your local bus terminal:

> Delaware Water Gap
> Wind Gap
> Palmerton
> port Clinton
> Clarks Ferry Bridge (U.S Rts. 22 &322)
> Duncannon
> U.S. Rt. 11-Cumberland Valley
> Caledonia State Park

Trying to arrange a hiking trip through your local bus agent can be a very frustrating experience. You will probably have to start from the beginning and explain exactly where you want to go and why. Then, since most trailheads are not scheduled stops, there will be the mattter of helping the agent determine precisely where on the route you want to be let off and/or picked up. Finally, when you actually board the bus, many of the same efforts will have to be expended again in explaining to the driver exactly what is wanted. Patient persistence is called for. Good luck!

Day Hikes and Short Hikes

There are several areas along the A.T. in Pennsylvania which provide opportunities for day hikes and short backpacking trips utilizing the A.T., side trails, and connecting trails. These trails are shown on the A.T. maps for Pennsylvania, and many of the important side trails are described in this guide. In addition, these trail systems and hikers using them are described in more detail in the following publications:

> **Pennsylvania Hiking Trails;** Keystone Trails Association; tenth edition; 1987. Order from KTA, Box 251, Cogan Station, PA 17728-0251.
>
> **Circuit Hikes in Virginia, West Virginia, Maryland, and Pennsylvania;** The Potomac Appalachian Trail Club. Order from PATC, 1718 N St., NW, Washington, D.C. 20036.

Some areas along the Pennsylvania A.T. which may be of particular interest in the planning of shorter hikes are listed below, along with the identifying Section number in each case:

The Pinnacle, Windsor Furnace, and Hawk Mountain Sanctuary. Section 4.

St. Anthony's Wilderness, Game Lands 210 and 211. Section 7.

Pole Steeple area. Section 12.

Pine Grove Furnace area. Sections 12 and 13.

Caledonia State Park area. Section 13.

PA BUREAU OF FORESTRY

39

Summary Of Distances

Miles N. to S. (Section)	Miles N. to S. (Cumulative)	Trail Feature	Miles S. to N. (Section)	Miles S. to N. (Cumulative)
Section 1				
0.0	0.0	I-80, Del. R. Bridge	15.3	229.7
4.7	4.7	Totts Gap	10.6	225.0
6.6	6.6	Kirkridge Shelter	8.7	223.1
7.2	7.2	Fox Gap, Rt. 191	8.1	222.5
8.8	8.8	Wolf Rocks	6.5	220.9
15.3	15.3	Wind Gap	0.0	214.4
Section 2				
0.0	15.3	Wind Gap	20.6	214.4
4.6	19.9	L.A. Smith Shelter	16.0	209.8
8.0	23.3	Smith Gap	12.6	206.4
15.5	30.8	Little Gap	5.1	198.9
20.6	35.9	Lehigh Gap, Rts 248 & 873	0.0	193.8
Section 3				
0.0	35.9	Lehigh Gap, Rts 248 & 873	15.3	193.8
0.7	36.6	Outerbridge Shelter	14.6	193.1
5.1	41.0	Lehigh Furnace Gap Rd.	10.2	188.7
8.4	44.3	Bake Oven Knob Shelter	6.9	185.4
9.5	45.4	Bake Oven Knob Road	5.8	184.3
13.3	49.2	New Tripoli Campsite	2.0	180.5
15.3	51.2	Blue Mountain Summit, Rt. 309	0.0	178.5
Section 4				
0.0	51.2	Blue Mountain Summit, Rt. 309	28.4	178.5
2.2	53.4	Jacksonville-Snyders Rd.	26.2	176.3
4.0	55.2	Allentown Shelter	24.4	174.5
5.5	56.7	Tri-County Corner	22.9	173.0
12.7	63.9	Eckville, Hawk Mt. Sanctuary	15.7	165.8
18.1	69.3	The Pinnacle	10.3	160.4
18.5	69.7	Trail to Blue Rocks Campground	9.9	160.0
22.1	73.3	Windsor Furnace Shelter	6.3	156.4
22.4	73.6	Windsor Furnace Campsite	6.0	156.1
25.1	76.3	Pocahontas Spring & Campsite	3.3	153.4
28.4	79.6	Port Clinton, Rt. 61	0.0	150.1

Miles N. to S. (Section)	Miles N. to S. (Cumulative)	Trail Feature	Miles S. to N. (Section)	Miles S. to N. (Cumulative)
Section 5				
0.0	79.6	Port Clinton, Rt. 61	15.0	150.1
6.9	86.5	Road to Shartlesville	8.1	143.2
8.8	88.4	Eagle Nest Shelter	6.2	141.3
15.0	94.6	Rt. 183	0.0	135.1
Section 6				
0.0	94.6	Rt. 183	18.2	135.1
3.5	98.1	Hertlein Campsite	14.7	131.6
5.0	99.6	Round Head/Showers Steps Trail	13.2	130.1
6.9	101.5	Rt. 501	11.3	128.2
8.5	103.1	Rt. 645	9.7	126.6
18.2	112.8	Swatara Gap	0.0	116.9
Section 7				
0.0	112.8	Swatara Gap	16.9	116.9
4.9	117.7	Game Land Maintenance Rd	12.0	112.0
5.7	118.5	Rausch Gap Shelter	11.2	111.2
8.0	120.8	Horse-Shoe Trail Junction	8.9	108.9
16.9	129.7	Clarks Valley, Rt. 325	0.0	100.0
Section 8				
0.0	129.7	Clarks Valley, Rt. 325	17.0	100.0
6.1	135.8	Peters Mountain Shelter	10.9	93.9
7.6	137.3	Zeager Shelter	9.4	92.4
9.2	138.9	Rt. 225	7.8	90.8
13.5	143.2	Clarks Ferry Shelter	3.5	86.5
17.0	146.7	Clarks Ferry Bridge	0.0	83.0
Section 9				
0.0	146.7	Clarks Ferry Bridge	14.7	83.0
5.6	152.3	Thelma Marks Memorial	9.1	77.4
10.6	157.3	Rt. 850	4.1	72.4
12.8	159.5	Darlington Shelter	1.9	70.2
14.7	161.4	Rt. 944	0.0	68.3
Section 10				
0.0	161.4	Rt. 944	10.7	68.3
4.4	165.8	Rt. 11	6.3	63.9
8.3	169.7	Rt. 641	2.4	60.0
10.7	172.1	Churchtown, Rt. 174	0.0	57.6

Miles N. to S. (Section)	Miles N. to S. (Cumulative)	Trail Feature	Miles S. to N. (Section)	Miles S. to N. (Cumulative)
Section 11				
0.0	172.1	Churchtown, Rt. 174	9.9	57.6
0.6	172.7	Rt. 74	9.3	57.0
1.6	173.7	Creek Rd.	8.3	56.0
2.6	174.7	Campbell Spring Shelter	7.3	55.0
7.0	179.1	Whiskey Spring Road	2.9	50.6
9.9	182.0	Rt. 94	0.0	47.7
Section 12				
0.0	182.0	Rt. 94	10.9	47.7
2.0	184.0	Rt. 34	8.9	45.7
2.8	184.8	Green Mountain Road	8.1	44.9
3.3	185.3	Tagg Run Shelters	7.6	44.4
10.9	192.9	Pine Grove Furnace State Park, Rt. 30	0.0	36.8
Section 13				
0.0	192.9	Pine Grove Furnace State Park, Rt. 30	19.7	36.8
2.0	194.9	High Mountain Road (Michaux Road)	17.7	34.8
3.4	196.3	Toms Run Shelters	16.3	33.4
8.4	201.3	Arendtsville-Shippensburg Road	11.3	28.4
9.6	202.5	Birch Run Shelters	10.1	27.2
12.1	205.0	Milesburn Cabin	7.6	24.7
17.1	210.0	Quarry Gap Shelters	2.6	19.7
19.7	212.6	Caledonia State Park, Rt. 30	0.0	17.1
Section 14				
0.0	212.6	Caledonia State Park, Rt. 30	17.1	17.1
4.6	217.2	Rt. 233	12.5	12.5
8.1	220.7	Hermitage Cabin	9.0	9.0
9.3	221.9	Tumbling Run Shelter	7.8	7.8
9.4	222.0	Antietam Rd./Shelter	7.7	7.7
14.4	227.0	Mackie Run Shelter	2.7	2.7
14.6	227.2	Rt. 16	2.5	2.5
17.1	229.7	Pen Mar	0.0	0.0

DETAILED TRAIL DESCRIPTION

Section 1

DELAWARE WATER GAP TO WIND GAP

DISTANCE   15.3 Miles

This section of Trail is maintained from the Delaware River to Fox Gap by the Springfield Trail Club, and from Fox Gap to Wind Gap by the BATONA Hiking Club.

GENERAL INFORMATION

Road Approaches

At some highways the A.T. is marked by an official signboard erected by the Pennsylvania Department of Transportation.

Road approaches to the Trail are as follows:

0.0 mi. at the Delaware River on the Pennsylvania side of the Interstate 80 bridge cannot be reached from I-80, since even brief parking on the bridge is not possible. Instead, enter Delaware Water Gap village on PA Rt. 611. At the intersection of Main Street and Mountain Road a large PennDOT sign notes the A.T. which comes in from I-80 on Delaware Avenue. This street deadends at the chain barrier on I-80 opposite a red brick highway maintenance building between the toll house and the bridge. A parking lot for hikers is located along the Trail 0.3 miles south of the bridge. See detailed Trail data.

7.2 mi. from the Delaware River in Fox Gap, PA Rt. 191 crosses between Bangor and Stroudsburg. A small parking area is located here.

15.3 mi. from the Delaware River, in Wind Gap, the Trail can be reached via the Wind Gap-Saylorsburg Road which passes under PA Rt. 33. The Trail is visible from Rt. 33 (a limited access highway) but can be reached only from the local traffic road. A small parking area is located adjacent to the A.T. sign.

Maps

Use KTA Section 1 Map which shows much Trail data, and is based on the following USGS 7½ quads: Stroudsburg, Saylorsburg, and Wind Gap.

Shelters

At 6.6 mi. from the Delaware River is the Kirkridge Shelter. Water is available at an outside tap toward the Kirkridge Retreat along a blue-blazed trail.

Public Accommodations

In Delaware Water Gap village there are motels, hotels, and restaurants. The Presbyterian Church of the Mountain, located just north of the Trail on Main Street, provides an information center for hikers. In Wind Gap, lodging may be obtained at the Gateway Motel, 100 yards north of the Gap. Lodging and restaurants are located in Wind Gap village down the south side of the mountain.

Supplies

Supplies can be obtained at several places in Delaware Water Gap village. The Pack Shack offers backpacking equipment and clothing, as well as repair services for equipment hikers carry. Supplies can be obtained at several places in Wind Gap village. A seasonal produce mart is located 100 yards north of Wind Gap, across from the motel.

General Description of the Trail

From an elevation of 300 feet in Delaware Water Gap, the trail climbs gradually for 2.6 miles to Mt. Minsi, with views of the river below and of the A.T. in New Jersey across the river. The trail generally keeps to the ridge except for slight dips into Totts Gap and Fox Gap and a deeper one into Wind Gap. From early summer on, this whole section is lacking in good springs. Points of interest along the trail are Lake Lenape, Council Rock, Winona Cliff (look for the profile of Chief Tammany on the mountain opposite), Lookout Rock, and Wolf Rocks. In the Wolf Rocks area use care and follow the blazes. The mountain top at this point is nearly one mile wide and the trail once lost, is difficult to find. Massive jumbled boulders are covered with rock tripe and other lichens. The view from Wolf Rocks is impressive.

Section 1

DELAWARE WATER GAP TO WIND GAP

NORTH TO SOUTH

Miles   **Detailed Trail Data**

0.0   From the Sidewalk on the PA side of the Interstate 80 bridge bear left on a path a short distance south of the toll house. This path enters a village street and in one block reaches Main St. (Pa. 611).

0.2   Cross Pa. 611 and continue ahead on Mountain Road.

0.3   Take the next fork to your left and continue on macadam.

0.4   Pass Lake Lenape on the right.

0.7   Bear left from gravel road.

0.9   Council Rock. Ascend with glimpses down to the highway and across to the river.

1.5   Winona Cliff--more views. Look for the profile of Chief Tammany across the river.

1.6   Cross brook and turn left, ascending.

1.7   Lookout Rock.

2.6   Summit of Mt. Minsi at 1480 ft. Trail follows a gravel road along the crest.

4.4   Turn left off road, then turn right through woods, passing to the south of communications towers.

4.7   Totts Gap. Cross road, trail now ascending through woods.

4.8   Cross twin power lines. Fine views.

6.5   Cross gravel road.

6.6   Blue-blazed trail leads to the **Kirkridge Shelter. WATER** is available at an outside tap toward the Kirkridge Retreat. Follow blue-blazed trail.

SECTION 1

- 6.8 Orange-blazed side trail to the left, known as "The Great Walk", descends mountain 0.8 miles to a replica of an early Celtic Christian Church.

- 7.2 Arrive at PA 191 in Fox Gap. Cross highway, pass under power lines and enter old woods road, then in 0.2 miles pass under telephone cable. There is a view north to Stroudsburg at the crest.

- 7.9 Trail turns right, joining woods road.

- 8.5 Trail turns left after passing under a power line. The roadway straight ahead continues to Cherry Valley

- 8.8 Reach Wolf Rocks, following the top edge before turning left. Use care to follow blazes. Once lost, the trail in this area is difficult to find.

- 10.0 A blue-blazed trail on the left leads down 0.3 miles to an unreliable spring.

- 13.4 Trail crosses a private road of the Blue Mountain Water Company affording a view, then meanders through varied forest.

- 14.7 Begin descent into Wind Gap.

- 15.3 Reach intersection with road from village of Wind Gap. To continue on A.T. turn right at official Appalachian Trail signboard, passing below the overpass carrying PA 33, a limited access highway.

Section 1

WIND GAP TO DELAWARE WATER GAP

SOUTH TO NORTH

Miles   Detailed Trail Data

- 0.0 At the official Appalachian Trail signboard in Wind Gap, ascend steeply from road onto trail through woods.

- 0.6 Reach height of land. Trail meanders through varied forest.

SECTION 1

- **1.9** Cross private road of Blue Mountain Water Company with good view. Continue along ridge top.

- **5.3** A blue-blazed trail on the right leads down 0.3 mi. to an unreliable spring.

- **6.5** Wolf Rocks. View ahead to Fox Gap and along Blue Mountain to Delaware Water Gap and beyond along Kittatinny Ridge in New Jersey. Trail turns right onto Wolf Rocks. Trail turns left and drops off the north side of the rocks.

- **6.8** Junction with old roadway which comes up from Cherry Valley on the left. Turn right on roadway and pass under power line.

- **7.4** Trail turns left leaving woods road.

- **7.9** Pass under a telephone cable. There is a view north to Stroudsburg at the crest.

- **8.1** Reach PA 191 in Fox Gap, crossing directly.

- **8.7** Blue-blazed trail leads to the **Kirkridge Shelter.** Excellent views to the south. **WATER** is available at an outside tap toward the Kirkridge Retreat. Follow blue-blazed trail.

- **8.8** Cross gravel road.

- **10.4** Cross two sets of power lines. Descend rocky trail.

- **10.6** Totts Gap. Trail bears right into woods, passing communication towers.

- **10.9** Turn left, then turn right onto gravel road.

- **12.7** Reach Mt. Minsi, 1480 ft. elevation. Begin descent by a series of switchbacks with excellent views of the Water Gap.

- **13.6** Lookout Rock.

- **13.7** Cross brook in rhododendron growth. Return to edge of escarpment.

- **13.8** Winona Cliff. Across the river the tilted strata of Mount Tammany is said to show the profile of Chief Tammany.

- **14.4** Council Rock. Take left fork at hemlock grove.

SECTION 1

14.6 Reach gravel road. Turn right downhill.

15.0 Pass Lake Lenape and hikers parking lot, and continue on paved road to village of Delaware Water Gap. Cross PA 611. Then in 50 feet turn right on dead-end street.

15.3 Reach Pennsylvania end of the Interstate 80 bridge.

   END OF NORTHERN DIVISION

To continue on A.T., cross Delaware River on this bridge to New Jersey.

Section 2

WIND GAP TO LEHIGH GAP

DISTANCE   20.6 Miles

This section of Trail is maintained by the Delaware Valley Chapter of the Appalachian Mountain Club from Wind Gap to Little Gap, and by the Philadelphia Trail Club from Little Gap to Lehigh Gap.

GENERAL INFORMATION

Road Approaches

At some highways the A.T. is marked by an official signboard erected by the Pennsylvania Department of Transportation. Road approaches to the Trail are as follows:

0.0 mi. In Wind Gap the Trail can be seen, but not reached from PA Rt. 33, a limited access highway. The local traffic road, from the village of Wind Gap over the mountain to Saylorsburg, passes under Rt. 33, and it is here in the gap that the Trail crosses. A small parking lot is adjacent.

8.0 mi. from Wind Gap, in Smith Gap, a jeep road crosses from Point Phillip to Kunkletown. Parking is available at a Game Commission parking lot located 0.3 mi. down the south side of the mountain. NOTE: Reports have been received of vandalism directed at cars parked in the Smith Gap area.

15.5 mi. from Wind Gap, in Little Gap, a road crosses from Danielsville (on PA 946) to the village of Little Gap (or Carbon) on U.S. 209. A Game Land parking lot is in the gap.

20.6 mi. from Wind Gap, in Lehigh Gap, the Trail crosses PA Rt. 248, and then crosses the Lehigh River on PA Rt. 873 bridge at a point 2 mi. south of Palmerton, PA. Access is from either end of bridge, with limited parking at both ends. Additional parking is available on the old railroad bed above the highway. Access is by a small entry road east of the traffic light.

SECTION 2
Maps

Use KTA Section 2 Map which shows much Trail data, and is based upon the following USGS quads: Wind Gap, Kunkletown, Palmerton.

Shelters

4.6 mi. from Wind Gap, on the side trail to Katellen, 0.1 mi. south of the A.T., is the Leroy A Smith Shelter, built by the AMC Delaware Valley Chapter in 1972. Spring is 0.2 mi. south. Sleeps six to eight.

Public Accommodations

In Wind Gap, lodging may be obtained at the Gateway Motel, 100 yds. north of the gap. At Palmerton, 2 mi. upstream, free overnight lodging with showers and cooking facilities are available in the Community Building. Hikers should apply at the Palmerton police station. Restaurants are available in Wind Gap, Danielsville, Palmerton, Walnutport, and Slatington.

Supplies

Supplies can be obtained in Wind Gap, Danielsville, Palmerton, Walnutport, and Slatington.

General Description of the Trail

The Trail is in State Game Lands most of the way, where overnight camping is permitted. (See introductory section on PA Game Lands.) After climbing out of Wind Gap, and passing Hahn's Lookout, the Trail stays on the ridge (crossing Smith Gap) until the dip and climb in Little Gap. From there, it traverses an open rocky area which gives impressive, if uninspiring, views of the railroads and Palmerton, industrial home of New Jersey Zinc Company. Close attention to the footway is advised in this area. Be sure to have a canteen of water since springs in the entire section are apt to be dry by early June most years.

Section 2

WIND GAP TO LEHIGH GAP

NORTH TO SOUTH

Miles   **Detailed Trail Data**

0.0   At a point 0.5 mi. north of Wind Gap village, just south of PA Rt. 33, is a parking lot on the east side of the local road. Trail crosses road and follows it north.

0.1   Pass under PA Rt. 33. Immediately beyond, bear left up wood and stone step switchbacks.

0.3   Cross pole line. Ascend gradually by switchbacks through woods.

0.8   Pass Lookout Rock. Views north over Saylorsburg, with Poconos in distance, and Aquashicola Creek in Chestnut Valley in foreground. From here, trail bears left to traverse the south side of Blue Mountain.

1.0   Hahn's Lookout. View south of Wind Gap village and South Mountain in the distance.

2.7   Cross underground pipeline.

4.4   Cross transmission line to tower. Good views north.

4.6   Pass blue-blazed Katellen Trail on left. AMC's Leroy A. Smith **SHELTER** at 0.1 mi. **SPRINGS** at 0.2, 0.4, and 0.5 mi. Paved road at 0.9 mi.

5.1   Cross white blazed PA Game Lands boundary. Use care. Boundary markings easily confused with A.T. blazes.

6.7   Bear right to northwest side of mountain on ridge top.

7.5   New relocation turns left off woods road.

8.0   Cross Smith Gap Road.

10.6   Pass blue-blazed Delps Trail on left (1.1 mi. to road). **SPRING** 0.3 mi. down side trail.

SECTION 2

11.7 Cross power line.

13.4 Trail turns left. Start of relocation away from Little Gap Ski area.

14.2 Trail turns left on old woods road.

14.5 Goose Knob. Views to the south and southwest.

14.7 Trail turns left, leaving woods road.

15.2 Weathering Knob. Views north. Trail starts down steep talus slope.

15.5 Cross hard road in Little Gap. To left, 1.5 mi., is Danielsville.

16.3 Cross a pipeline.

16.5 Cross under high tension lines. Height of land to your left offers superior view.

16.8 Side trail to right leads 250 feet to a variable **SPRING.**

18.8 Open area. Very rocky.

19.3 Turn left, cross rock slide, and descend steeply. (Straight ahead is a blue-blazed winter trail which offers a longer but more gradual and sheltered descent, rejoining A.T. in the gap.

20.2 Cross PA Rt. 248 at its junction (traffic light) with PA Rt. 145; turn right on pavement to PA Rt. 873 at east end of the highway bridge across Lehigh River. To the right, 2.0 mi., is Palmerton; to the left, 2.5 mi., are Walnutport and Slatington.

20.6 Cross to west end of bridge. To continue, turn right from highway, passing billboards, then ascending between billboards and house.

Section 2

LEHIGH GAP TO WIND GAP

SOUTH TO NORTH

Miles   Detailed Trail Data

0.0   From west end of PA Rt. 873 highway bridge across Lehigh River, cross bridge to east end, then turn right along PA Rt. 248.

0.4   Cross PA Rt. 248 at its junction (traffic light) with PA Rt. 145, and turn left along highway for 100 yds. Then turn right up embankment. Cross old railroad bed. Turning right, ascend first gradually, then steeply, crossing shoulder of ridge of Blue Mountain with fine views. Cross rock slide with grade becoming easier. (A blue-blazed winter trail continues along the old railroad bed for some distance; then turns right up the mountain, offering a more gradual and sheltered ascent. Rejoins A.T. at 1.3 mi.

1.3   Bear right. Trail continues to be rocky, following old survey line on top of mountain. Blue-blazed trail comes in on left.

1.8   Open area. Trail follows an old dirt road.

3.8   Side trail leads left 250 ft. to intermittent **SPRING.**

4.1   Cross under high tension lines. Height of land to your right offers superior views.

4.3   Cross pipeline.

5.1   Cross paved road in Little Gap. To the right, 1.5 mi., is Danielsville. Trail crosses bog, then up steep talus slope.

5.4   Weathering Knob. Views north and northwest.

5.7   Trail turns right.

5.9   Trail turns right on old road; starts climb.

6.1   Goose Knob. Views to the south and southwest.

6.4   Trail leaves old road and enters woods.

- 7.2 Trail turns right.
- 9.0 Cross power line.
- 10.0 Pass blue-blazed Delps Trail on right (1.1 mile to road). **SPRING** 0.3 mi. down side trail.
- 12.6 Cross Smith Gap Road.
- 12.8 Trail turns right on woods road.
- 13.9 Trail bears right, crossing flat to southeast side. Use care for the next two miles. Do not be confused by Game Lands boundary markings.
- 16.0 Pass blue-blazed Katellen Trail on right. AMC's Leroy A. Smith **SHELTER** at 0.1 mi. **SPRINGS** at 0.2, 0.4, and 0.5 mi. Road at 0.9 mi.
- 16.2 Fine view north at power line.
- 17.9 Cross clearing of underground pipeline.
- 19.6 Pass Hahn's Lookout. View south to Wind Gap village and South Mountain in the distance. Trail bears right to south side of mountain.
- 19.8 Lookout Rocks with fine views of the Poconos in the distance to the north. In the foreground is Chestnut Valley through which flows beautiful Aquashicola Creek. Trail ascends by switchbacks.
- 20.3 Cross pole line.
- 20.5 Descend last switchback with stone steps. Pass under PA Rt. 33 bridge.
- 20.6 Cross road to A.T. sign and parking lot.

Section 3

LEHIGH GAP TO PA RT. 309

DISTANCE   15.3 Miles

This section of the trail is maintained by the Philadelphia Trail Club from Lehigh Gap to Lehigh Furnace Gap Road; by the Blue Mountain Eagle Climbing Club from Lehigh Furnace Gap Road to Bake Oven Knob road; and by the Allentown Hiking Club from Bake Oven Knob Road to PA Rt. 309.

GENERAL INFORMATION

Road Approaches

At some highways the A.T. is marked by an official signboard erected by the Pennsylvania Department of Transportation.

Road approaches to the trail are as follows:

0.0 mi. in Lehigh Gap, this section begins at the west end of the PA Rt. 873 bridge over the Lehigh River, two miles below Palmerton. Parking is limited. (See Section 2)

5.1 mi. from Lehigh Gap, access by Lehigh Furnace Gap Road between Lehigh Furnace and Ashfield. Parking under transmission lines.

9.5 mi. from Lehigh Gap, access by Bake Oven Knob Road between Germansville and Andreas. Game Commission parking lot.

15.3 from Lehigh Gap, access by PA Rt. 309 at Blue Mountain Summit. There is a Game Commission parking lot just north of the trail where it reaches PA Rt. 309 from the north.

Maps

Use KTA Section Three Map which shows much trail data, and is based upon the following USGS 7 1/2" quads; Palmerton, Lehighton, Slatedale, and New Tripoli.

Shelters

0.7 mi. from Lehigh Gap is the George W. Outerbridge Shelter for ten, located directly along the trail. Spring is passed before reaching shelter.

8.4 mi. from Lehigh Gap is the Bake Oven Knob Shelter for six, located just south of the trail. Variable springs are located down the hill on a blue-blazed trail at 100 yds. and 200 yds.

Public Accommodations

In Palmerton--in addition to motels, hotels and restaurants--free overnight lodging with shower and cooking facilities is available in the Community Building. Hikers should apply at the Palmerton police station. There is an excellent German restaurant at PA 309.

Supplies

Supplies can be obtained in nearby Palmerton, Walnutport, and Slatington.

General Description of the Trail

The trail climbs steadily to the Outerbridge Shelter, beyond which the A.T. (South Trail) continues straight ahead, while the blue-blazed North Trail goes to the ridge top. The North Trail is more scenic, but open to winter storms. A point of interest off the North Trail is Devil's Pulpit, overlooking the Lehigh River. The A.T. then passes through Game Lands and dips to Lehigh Furnace Gap. Game Land boundary blazes are often confused with A.T. Blazes but are of erratic size and location. USE CAUTION. Climbing again, the trail leads to Bake Oven Knob with its commanding view of fertile farmland below, and its reputation as a birdwatcher's vantage point during the fall hawk migrations. The trail passes Bear Rocks with 360 degree views, and then crosses a knife edge known as "The Cliffs." This is one of the most scenic sections of the A.T. in Pennsylvania.

Section 3

LEHIGH GAP TO PA RT. 309

NORTH TO SOUTH

Miles   **Detailed Trail Data**

0.0   At the west end of the PA Rt. 873 highway bridge across the Lehigh River, turn right leaving the highway, passing a billboard on the right.

0.1   Pass Stone Boy Scout marker to your left on the highway bank. Trail turns right up old road between the billboard and a house on your left.

0.2   Pass under power lines. Watch for blaze across swath.

0.6   Pass piped **SPRING** on right.

0.7   Reach the George W. Outherbridge **SHELTER** on right, with space for up to ten. Turn right around shelter, and proceed up the mountain.

0.8   A.T. continues straight ahead, slabbing the southeast side of the mountain. This is known locally as the South Trail. Blue-blazed trail to the right, the North Trail, goes to the top of the mountain and rejoins the A.T. at 2.4 mi. The North Trail is more scenic, but is open to winter storms. It passes another blue-blazed side trail in 0.3 mi., which drops steeply to devil's Pulpit with good views of the gap. The North Trail, which will eventually become the A.T., continues on to the ridge, passing a TV tower before rejoining the A.T.

2.4   West junction of the South and North Trails.

2.6   Pass over the Northeast Extension of the Pennsylvania Turnpike, which goes through the mountain far below. The town of Jim Thorpe can be seen to the north.

3.8   Rock outcrop on the left. Good views.

4.1   Trail follows State Game Land boundary.

SECTION 3

4.8 Trail turns left into State Game Lands.

5.1 Arrive at Lehigh Furnace Gap Road, passable by auto. Trail turns right onto road. To the left, south, 0.7 mi. down the hill, along the road, is a piped **SPRING**.

5.2 Trail goes left from the road and up under a power line into a woods road.

5.4 Trail goes right, leaving woods road.

6.6 Rock outcrop gives views to the north.

8.4 Pass Bake Oven Knob **SHELTER** and campsite on south side just below the A.T. Blue-blazed trail from the shelter leads down hill past an often dry **SPRING** on right and then to a second **SPRING** on the right in another 200 yds. This trail continues to Bake Oven Knob Road and then to a paved road in the valley in 2.0 mi.

8.7 Ascend ridge steeply over a rock slide.

9.1 Bake Oven Knob, elevation 1,560 ft. site of former air beacon. To the left is exceptional lookout with 180 degree views to south. To the right is view north.

9.5 Cross Game Commission parking lot and Bake Oven Knob Road, passable by auto. Continue along summit, following a grassy road.

9.9 Turn left where road forks.

10.9 Blue-blazed trail to the right climbs to Bear Rocks with fine 360 degree views. Don't miss it.

11.2 Trail crosses the knife edge known as "The Cliffs."

13.3 Cross under power line. A blue-blazed trail to the right descends the power line to base of valley in 0.2 mi., and then right 200 yds. to New Tripoli **CAMPSITE** and **SPRING**.

15.3 Reach PA Rt. 309 at Blue Mountain Summit, elevation 1,360 ft. Turn right onto highway and then turn left crossing restaurant parking lot.

Section 3

PA RT. 309 TO LEHIGH GAP

SOUTH TO NORTH

Miles   **Detailed Trail Data**

0.0   From the restaurant, turn right on PA Rt. 309 (south) over the crest of Blue Mountain, elevation 1,360 ft.

0.1   Turn left onto an eroded woods road.

0.3   At intersection, turn right, then bear left.

0.9   Reach the ridge, continuing along woods road.

2.2   At the power line the road becomes a trail and the footway becomes rocky. A blue-blazed trail to the left descends the power line to base of valley in 0.2 mi., and then right 200 yds. to New Tripoli **CAMPSITE** and **SPRING.**

3.3   Trail turns left, following the knife edge known as "The Cliffs" with a view ahead to Bear Rocks.

4.4   Blue-blazed trail to the left climbs 50 yds. to Bear Rocks, with 360 degree views. Don't miss it.

5.0   Bear right on fork at grassy road.

5.4   Reach Bake Oven Knob Road, a cross-mountain gravel road passable by autos. Trail passes throuh Game Commission parking lot.

6.2   Pass over summit of Bake Oven Knob, 1,560 ft. elevation. Note remains of old air beacon. To the right is exceptional lookout with 180 degree views to south. To the left is view north. Reach rock slide on north side of mountain. Cross slide using care.

6.9   Bake Oven Knob **SHELTER** and **CAMPSITE** is on south side of trail just below A.T. Blue-blazed trail leads down past often dry **SPRING** on right, and second **SPRING** 200 yds. further down on right. Trail then leads 0.7 mi. to Bake Oven Road. It is then 1.1 mi. to paved road valley.

SECTION 3

- **8.7** Fine view to north where trail follows outcrop.
- **9.0** Cross rocky crest to north side of mountain.
- **10.2** Cross transmission line and bear right on Lehigh Furnace Gap cross-mountain road, passable for autos. Turn left on top into woods road at radio tower.
- **10.5** Trail turns right following Game Lands boundary line.
- **11.2** Trail turns left, away from Game Lands, and crosses an abandoned telephone line.
- **11.5** Pass large rock outcrop on right. Rough trail to top of rocks gives superb views.
- **12.7** Pass over Northeast Extension of Pennsylvania Turnpike which goes through tunnel far below.
- **12.9** Trail junction of blue-blazed North Trail which goes to the left for 2.4 mi., and the A.T. (South Trail) which goes to the right. The North Trail follows the crest of Blue Mountain and is the more scenic route, but it is open to winter storms. Two miles along the North Trail there is another blue-blazed side trail leading downhill 0.4 mi. to Devil's Pulpit, with good views of the Lehigh Gap. The A.T. (South Trail) slabs down the southeast side of the mountain. The North Trail will eventually become the A.T.
- **14.5** East junction of the South and North Trails.
- **14.6** Pass George W. Outerbridge **SHELTER** on left, with space for up to ten. A.T. bears left around shelter, passing piped **SPRING** in 150 yds.
- **15.1** Continue to descend, passing under power lines with views into the gap.
- **15.3** Arrive at west end of highway bridge over Lehigh River (PA Rt. 873). Notice the Boy Scout monument on your right along macadam road at the end of the section.

To continue on A.T., cross Lehigh River Bridge.

Section 4

PA RT. 309 TO PORT CLINTON

DISTANCE   28.4 Miles

This section of the trail is maintained by the Allentown Hiking Club from PA 309 to Tri-County Corner and by the Blue Mountain Eagle Climbing Club from Tri-County Corner to Port Clinton.

GENERAL INFORMATION

Road Approaches

At some highways the A.T. is marked by an official signboard erected by the Pennsylvania Department of Transportation.

Road approaches to the trail are as follows:

0.0 mi. at PA Rt. 309. There is a Game Commission parking lot just north of the trail on the east side of the highway.

2.1 mi. from PA Rt. 309, access by the Jacksonville-Snyders cross-mountain road. This is a rough stone mountain road, which is passable by auto, but better suited to trucks and jeeps. This road can be pinpointed on KTA Section Four Map. Limited parking.

12.7 mi. from PA Rt. 309, in the village of Eckville, the trail crosses an unnumbered road between the villages of Kempton, on PA Rt. 143, and Drehersville, on PA Rt. 895. This road is the access road to Hawk Mountain Sanctuary. Parking is available at a Game Commission lot on the right side of southbound unimproved Pine Swamp Road, 0.5 mi. from Eckville, and 0.25 mi. from the A.T. on a blue-blazed trail.

28.4 mi. from PA Rt. 309, the trail crosses a macadam road within sight of PA Rt. 61, 0.5 mi. south of the village of Port Clinton. Parking is available on both sides of the side road. This crossing is marked by an official sign erected by the Pennsylvania Department of Transportation. The trail then proceeds south under PA Rt. 61 and along the Schuylkill River.

SECTION 4
Maps

Use KTA Section Four Map, which shows much trail data, and is based upon the following USGS 7½" quads: New Tripoli, New Ringgold, Hamburg, and Auburn.

Shelters

4.0 mi. from Blue Mountain Summit is the Allentown Hiking Club Shelter for six. A spring is nearby.

20.4 mi. from Blue Mountain Summit is the Windsor Furnace Shelter. A spring and outhouse are established nearby. See detailed trail data for directions.

Public Accommodations

Overnight or weekend lodging is available for hikers at the Y.W.C.A. Blue Mountain Camp, Hamburg, PA. **DONATION REQUESTED.** Meals are available during the camp season, usually June 9 through the end of August. At other times of the year, prior arrangement must be made with the camp caretaker by calling 215/562-8691 or writing to Camp Director, Y.W.C.A., 8th and Washington Sts., Reading, PA, 19601. The camp is one mile south of the A.T. on a blue-blazed side trail from Pocohontas Spring.

The Port Clinton Hotel, 0.5 mi. north of the trail on PA Rt. 61, provides lodging for hikers. Accommodations and restaurant are available in Hamburg, PA, three miles south of Port Clinton, PA Rt. 61.

Supplies

Supplies can be purchased in Hamburg, PA. There are no grocery stores in either Eckville or Port Clinton.

General Description of the Trail

From Blue Mountain Summit at PA Rt. 309, the trail stays on the ridge, with slight climbs to the Allentown Shelter and at Tri-County Corner. Then a rather sharp descent leads to Eckville. The footway is rocky all the way. Leaving Eckville, the trail climbs gradually and then steeply before leveling out on the ridge leading to the spectacular Pinnacle. A drop again into Windsor Furnace, and another climb precede the steep descent into Port Clinton. Points of interest along the way are Tri-County Corner with its 360 degree views, Dan's Pulpit, The Pinnacle, Pulpit Rock, Windsor Furnace and numerous charcoal hearths, such as the one at Pocohontas Spring. These hearths supplied fuel for the furnace. A special point of interest is the Hawk Mountain Sanctuary near Eckville. This is a world-renowned wildlife refuge, and the first sanctuary in the world to offer protection to birds of prey. The Sanctuary Headquarters Building contains a series of exhibits and is staffed by professional curators who live at the Sanctuary. See the special section in the front of this book for more information about Hawk Mountain Sanctuary.

Section 4

PA RT. 309 TO PORT CLINTON

NORTH TO SOUTH

Miles   Detailed Trail Data

0.0   From PA Rt. 309 at Blue Mountain Summit, turn left across the parking lot of the restaurant, entering a Game Commission road.

1.9   Bear left upgrade and in 100 yds. turn right.

2.2   Reach the cross-mountain road, connecting the villages of Jacksonville and Snyders, and enter a woods road.

3.4   Turn sharp right uphill.

4.0   Blue-blazed trail to the left leads 300 yds. to a **SPRING** and the Allentown Hiking Club **SHELTER,** but this trail is very rocky. It is better to take the next blue-blazed trail to the left which leads 30 yds. to the same shelter. **Spring may be dry in dry summers,** but water can always be found by following the yellow-blazed trail down the south side of the mountain to another spring.

SECTION 4

4.4 Turn left off woods road. Trail becomes rocky.

5.5 Reach Tri-County Corner. A blue-blazed trail leads left, down the Old Dresher Road, not passable for autos, 1.8 mi. to the valley floor, The A.T. turns right upgrade on the Old Dresher Road. A blue-blazed trail to the right leads a short distance to the top of the rock pile where a marker indicates the intersection of Berks, Lehigh, and Schuylkill Counties. Excellent views. Tri-County Corner is the place where, in 1926, construction was first begun on the Appalachian Trail in Pennsylvania by a work party from the Blue Mountain Eagle Climbing Club.

5.7 Turn left on woods road.

6.6 Balanced Rock on left, Good views.

7.3 Blue-blazed trail to the left leads steeply downhill 90 yds. to Dan's **SPRING, not dependable.**

8.2 Blue-blazed trail to left leads 1.9 mi. into the valley, passing **SPRING** at 3/4 mi.

9.3 A few feet to the left of the trail is Dan's Pulpit, named in honor of Daniel K. Hoch, one of the founders of the Blue Mountain Eagle Climbing Club.

9.9 Turn left on old woods road.

10.4 A.T. turns sharp left down the hill. A blue-blazed trail to the right leads 2 mi. to Hawk Mountain Sanctuary's North Lookout, and then to the headquarters and museum. A fee is charged to hike in the sanctuary. **NO CAMPING IS PERMITTED.**

11.0 Turn right on footpath.

11.6 Turn right on old A.T. Trail becomes rocky and gullied.

12.1 Turn right again uphill.

12.2 Turn right, then left, and come to log walkway and bridge over swamp and creek. Bear left, then sharp right.

12.4 Turn right on old logging road.

12.7 Cross hard surfaced road. Right leads to Hawk Mountain Sanctuary; left to Eckville.

12.9 Crossing of woods roads. Turn left.

13.1 Turn off woods road to left.

13.3 Turn left, disregarding Game Lands boundary blazes.

13.5 Bear right off woods road. Old A.T. is now a blue-blazed trail to Game Lands parking lot, 0.25 mi.

14.5 Panther **SPRING,** always running, on right.

15.5 At junction of woods roads, A.T. turns left.

EXCEPT AS NOTED IN THIS GUIDE, NO CAMPING OR FIRES ARE ALLOWED IN THIS AREA WHICH IS THE HAMBURG BOROUGH WATERSHED

16.1 Reliable Gold **SPRING** 30 yds. on right. **No camping or fires.**

16.4 Keep left where woods road goes right.

17.1 Keep left where old woods road goes to the right.

17.4 At clearing, keep to the left.

17.8 Pass through a charcoal hearth.

18.1 Blue-blazed trail to the left leads 80 yds. to the spectacular Pinnacle, 1,635 ft. elevation. This is considered by many to be **the most spectacular vista** along the A.T. in Pennsylvania. There are two caves below the Pinnacle, and many sheer cliffs to explore. A.T. turns sharply to the right. **NO CAMPING OR FIRES ALLOWED.**

18.5 Yellow-blazed trail to the left leads down a steep hill for 1.3 mi. to Blue Rocks. In another 0.2 mi. is the Blue Rocks Campground, privately owned, where **SUPPLIES** can be purchased at the camp store.

19.6 Trail crosses a rock field.

19.7 Pass through cleft in rock formation.

19.8 Rock field 10 yds. to the right with a view to the north.

20.0 Excellent view to the left on a rock outcropping.

20.1 Pass tower on right.

20.2 Pulpit Rock on the left at 1,582 ft. elevation, with excellent views of the Pinnacle to the left and Blue Rocks in the foreground.

NO CAMPING OR FIRES ALLOWED EXCEPT AS NOTED IN THIS GUIDE.

20.3 Pass around the Astronomical Park of the Lehigh Valley Amateur Astronomical Society.

20.4 Trail bears left decending mountain on an old woods road.

22.1 Blue-blazed trail to the right leads 500 ft. to the Windsor Furnace **SHELTER.** Limited camping permitted around the shelter.

22.3 Trail, now on a road, crosses Furnace Creek, **DO NOT swim or bathe in creek.**

22.4 Arrive at Windsor Furnace, site of an early pig iron works. The remains of the old engine foundation are in the undergrowth. An essential ingredient was charcoal, and the trail passes many flat round charcoal hearths, or burning sites, 30 to 50 ft. in diameter.

The Borough of Hamburg has provided **CAMPSITES** 500 yds. south on a blue-blazed trail. The sites are located beyond the Reservoir buildings on a dirt road to the left. Water may be obtained from the stream at the campsites.

NO OTHER CAMPING IS ALLOWED, EXCEPT AS NOTED.

The A.T. goes left on an old woods road.

23.2 Take right fork from woods road. Use care.

23.9 Intermittent **SPRING,** dry in summer.

25.1 Pocohontas **SPRING,** good all year. A blue-blazed trail to the left leads 1 mi. to the Y.W.C.A. Blue Mountain Camp.

25.2	Reach ridge and bear left.
25.9	Cross clearing for telephone line.
26.1	Cross Game Lands boundary line.
26.9	Reach top of ridge. Views to the left of Schuylkill River valley and dam.
27.2	Descend on switchbacks.
27.6	Road crossing and parking area.
27.7	Turn right under PA Rt.61 highway bridge. Bear right along Schuylkill River.
28.2	Turn left on Penn St., Port Clinton.
28.3	Turn left on Broad St. and cross Little Schuylkill River.
28.4	Turn left and cross Schuylkill River on railroad bridge. Parking on Port Clinton streets is limited. Use area east of PA Rt. 61, 0.5 mi. south of village.

Section 4

PORT CLINTON TO PA RT. 309

SOUTH TO NORTH

Miles   **Detailed Trail Data**

0.0	Cross the Schuylkill River on a railroad bridge.
0.1	Reach Broad St. in Port Clinton and turn right. Limited parking on streets. Use area east of PA Rt. 61, 0.5 mi. south of village.
0.2	Turn right on Penn St. and then bear right into woods along Schuylkill River.
0.7	Bear left and cross under PA Rt. 61.
0.8	Cross macadam side road at parking area and begin ascent to the right.

SECTION 4

1.2 Ascend on switchbacks. Fine views of Schuylkill River and dam near Hamburg.

1.5 Reach top of ridge at rock outcropping. Descend left.

2.3 Cross Game Lands boundary. Be careful to continue straight ahead on trail.

2.5 Cross clearing for telephone line.

3.2 Bear right and descend from ridge.

3.3 Pocohontas **SPRING.** A blue-blazed trail to the right leads 1.0 mi. to the Y.W.C.A. Blue Mountain Camp.

3.7 Bear left where road forks.

4.6 Pass **SPRING, frequently dry.**

6.0 Enter lands of the Hamburg Borough Watershed.

**NO FIRES OR CAMPING ALLOWED
EXCEPT AS NOTED IN THIS GUIDE**

Arrive at the site of Windsor Furnace, an early pig iron works. Note glassy slag in the footpath. A blue-blazed trail to the right leads 500 yds. to a **CAMPSITE** provided by the Hamburg Water Authority. Sites are located beyond the buildings on a dirt road to the left. WATER may be obtained at the stream behind the campsites.

EXCEPT AS NOTED, THIS IS THE ONLY CAMPING PERMITTED IN THE WATERSHED.
NO SWIMMING IS PERMITTED IN THE CREEK OR IN THE IMPOUNDMENT.

A.T. goes straight ahead.

6.1 Trail, now on a road, crosses Furnace Creek and bears right onto a woods road. **NO SWIMMING OR BATHING PERMITTED.**

6.2 Turn right where a blue-blazed trail to the left leads 500 ft. to the Windsor Furnace **SHELTER.** Limited camping permitted around shelter.

6.3 Trail ascends Blue Mountain gradually, then steeply.

8.1 Pass around Astronomical Park of the Lehigh Valley Amateur Astronomical Society.

8.2 Pulpit Rock, elevation 1,582 ft. Excellent view of the Pinnacle to the left, with Blue Rocks in the foreground. **NO CAMPING OR FIRES ALLOWED.**

8.3 Pass tower on left.

8.6 Rock field 10 yds. to the left with views to the north.

8.7 Pass through cleft in rock formation.

9.9 Yellow-blazed trail to the right leads down a steep hill for 1.3 mi. to Blue Rocks. In another 0.2 mi. is the Blue Rocks Campground, privately owned, where **SUPPLIES** can be purchased.

10.3 Blue-blazed side trail to the right leads 80 yds. to the spectacular Pinnacle, 1,635 ft. elevation. Many consider this the most worthwhile and scenic viewpoint along the A.T. in Pennsylvania. There are two caves, and many sheer clifts to explore. A.T. turns sharply to the left. **NO CAMPING OR FIRES ALLOWED.**

10.6 Pass through a charcoal hearth.

11.0 At clearing, keep to the right.

11.3 A.T. bears right where old woods road goes left.

12.0 Keep right where woods road goes left to Furnace Creek.

12.3 Reliable Gold **SPRING** 30 yds. on left. **NO CAMPING OR FIRES.**

12.9 Junction of trails. A.T turns right toward Eckville.

13.2 Reach crest. Disregard the white boundary blazes of the Game Lands. Trail turns left descending.

13.5 Bear right, disregarding grassy woods road to the left.

13.9 Panther **SPRING** on the left. Continue descending on the old Windsor Furnace Road through Game Lands.

SECTION 4

14.9 Bear left off road. Old A.T. is now a blue-blazed trail to the Game Lands parking lot, 0.25 mi.

15.0 Turn left uphill.

15.1 Disregard Game Lands blazes. Turn right.

15.3 Another woods road. Turn off road to your right.

15.4 Sharp left uphill, then continue on logging road.

15.5 Crossing of woods roads; turn right.

15.7 Cross hard surfaced road. Right leads to Eckville, left to Hawk Mountain Sanctuary, a very desirable side trip. **NO CAMPING PERMITTED AT THE SANCTUARY.**

16.0 Left on old logging road.

16.2 Left off road, then sharp right. Come to bridge and walkway over creek and swamp. After swamp, turn right, then left.

16.3 Left again uphill.

16.7 Reach log bridge across gully.

16.8 Turn left. Trail becomes rocky and gullied.

17.4 Turn left onto abandoned cross-mountain road, climbing to the ridge.

18.0 Blue-blazed trail to the left leads 2 mi. to Hawk Mountain's North Lookout. A fee is charge to hike in the Sanctuary. **NO CAMPING PERMITTED AT THE SANCTUARY.**

18.5 Leave old mountain road and turn right on foot trail.

19.1 Pass rock outcrop know as Dan's Pulpit where hiking's grand old man, Danny Hoch, conducted Sunday services. Fine views at 1,600 ft. elevation.

20.2 Blue-blazed trail to right leads 1.9 mi. into the valley, passing **SPRING** at 3/4 mi.

21.1 Blue-blazed trail to the right leads downhill 90 yds. to Dan's **SPRING. May be dry** in dry weather.

Mile	
21.8	Balanced Rock to the right of trail. Fine views.
22.9	Arrive at the Old Dresher Road and turn right, descending. A blue-blazed trail to the left leads a short distance to the top of the rock pile where there is a marker denoting the intersection of Berks, Lehigh, and Schuylkill Counties. Excellent views. Tri-County Corner is the site of the very first blazing of the Appalachian Trail in Pennsylvania, in 1926, by a crew from the Blue Mountain Eagle Climbing Club.
23.4	A.T. turns left into the woods. Trail becomes very rocky. Blue-blazed trail straight ahead on the Old Dresher Road leads 1.8 mi. into the valley.
24.0	Turn right on woods road.
24.2	Blue-blazed trail to the right leads 30 yds. to the Allentown Hiking Club **SHELTER** for six. This trail leads on another 300 yds. to a **SPRING** and then connects to the A.T. The **spring may be dry** in dry weather, but water can always be found by followig the yellow-blazed trail down the mountain to another spring.
24.4	Blue-blazed trail from the shelter rejoins the A.T.
26.2	Cross the Jacksonville-Snyders Road, passable by auto.
26.5	Turn left descending. Reach old road in 80 yds. and then right upgrade.
28.4	Arrive at Blue Mountain Summit on PA Rt. 309, passing a restaurant. Turn right along the highway.
	In 0.1 mi. cross the highway.

Section 5

PORT CLINTON TO PA RT. 183

DISTANCE   15.0 Miles

This section of the trail is maintained by the Blue Mountain Eagle Climbing Club.

GENERAL INFORMATION

Road Approaches

At some highways the A.T. is marked by an official signboard erected by the Pennsylvania Department of Transportation.

Road Approaches to the trail are as follows:

0.0 mi. Parking is available on the side road which starts east of PA Rt. 61, 0.5 mi. south of the town of Port Clinton, 0.8 mi. from the parking area at the south end of the Schuylkill Railroad bridge to the west of PA Rt. 61 in Port Clinton. The bridge is 0.1 mi. from the Canal Museum.

15.0 mi. from Port Clinton, the trail crosses PA Rt. 183 between Strausstown and Summit Station. There is a Game Commission parking lot 0.2 mi. south of the mountaintop on the east side of the road.

Maps

Use KTA Secton Five Map, which shows much trail data, and is based upon the following USGS 7 1/2" quads: Auburn and Friedensburg.

Shelters

8.8 mi. from Port Clinton is Eagle Nest **SHELTER** for eight. Yeich **SPRING** nearby.

SECTION 5

Public Accommodations

In Port Clinton is the Port Clinton Hotel where hikers can secure lodging. The Peanut Shop provides snacks. In Shartlesville there are several famous eating places serving family style meals. In Hamburg there are hotels and motels.

Supplies

There are grocery stores in Hamburg, three miles south of Port Clinton, and Shartlesville.

General Description of the Trail

The trail begins with a steep climb out of Port Clinton, gaining 1,000 feet in two miles. The footway is quite rocky for most of the first six miles. Beyond, the trail passes through a maturing forest which is surprisingly rock-free, and altogether pleasant hiking. The Game Commission adminstrative road, over which the trail was previously routed, is crossed twice before reaching PA Rt 183.

Section 5

PORT CLINTON TO PA RT. 183

NORTH TO SOUTH

Miles Detailed Trail Data

- 0.0 Leaving bridge, immediately turn left along the railroad tracks. Cross the Schuylkill River on the railroad bridge. Continue on cinder road to a double blaze.

- 0.3 Turn right across tracks and climb bank to old single railroad bed. Continue left on track for about 150 ft.

- 0.6 Turn right on old road which switches back, ascending and becoming a woods path.

- 1.2 Cross old pipeline.

- 1.6 Cross new pipeline.

SECTION 5

1.7 Come to Dynamite Road. A.T. turns sharp right here. Footway becomes rocky. Blue-blazed trail to left leads to Mountain Road at the foot of the ridge.

2.3 Cross Game Lands road.

2.6 Come to Game Lands road. Follow road to the right (but do not cross) for about 45 yds. and reenter woods.

2.7 Reach Auburn Lookout, a rock outcrop off the trail to the right. Excellent view of Auburn village and surrounding area.

3.4 Cross Marshalls Path. Blue-blazed trail to the left leads to Mountain Road in Bellmans Gap at the foot of the ridge.

3.6 Come to Game Lands road. Cross diagonally, following arrows, cairns, and blazes for about 120 yds. Enter woods on trail which is now south of the road.

4.8 Pass Phillip's Canyon **SPRING** trail on the left. Spring is 135 yds. down a steep descent and is **sometimes dry.**

5.6 Come to Game Lands road. Cross directly, following arrows, cairns and blazes for about 100 yds. Trail enters woods and is now on the north side of the road. Soon begin descent from the ridge on rock steps.

6.0 At bottom of ridge turn left. Follow trail with improved footway through the woods.

6.5 A.T. bears right.

6.9 Cross old mountain road. To the left are Game Lands parking lot; 1.6 mi. and Shartlesville, 3.6 mi.

SECTION 5

- 8.8 Come to blue-blazed Trail leading right to Eagles Nest **SHELTER**. Water available at nearby Yeich **SPRING**.

- 8.9 Cross Game Lands boundary. Leave Weiser State Forest.

- 9.1 Cross Game Commission Administrative Road. Continue on trail.

- 9.7 Cross Sand Spring Trail. Sand **SPRING,** a fine walled spring, is located 0.2 mi. to the left. **No camping** is permitted at or near the spring.

- 10.8 Reach junction of A.T., Eagles Nest, and Little Creek side trails. A.T. continues across junction.

- 11.0 Trail turns right off obscure Game Lands road.

- 12.5 Cross small stream.

- 13.6 Blue-blazed trail to left leads 200 yds. to Black Swatara **SPRING. No Camping.**

- 14.4 Cross Game Commission Administrative road. Game Lands parking lot is at the foot of this road adjacent to PA Rt. 183.

- 14.6 Turn right onto trail, leaving woods road.

- 15.0 Pass Rentschler marker, 15 yds. to the right, erected in honor of Dr. H. F. Rentschler, who beginning in 1926, led the work parties which originally established the A.T. between the Lehigh and Susquehanna Rivers. Reach PA Rt. 183. Game Lands Parking lot, 0.2 mi. to the south, off to the left.

   To continue on A.T., cross PA Rt.183 and ascend bank.

Section 5

PA RT. 183 TO PORT CLINTON

SOUTH TO NORTH

Miles   Detailed Trail Data

0.0   Trail crosses PA Rt. 183 at official PennDOT highway sign marking the A.T. Trail follows road up slight incline and immediately passes Rentschler marker, 15 yds. off to the left. Dr. H.F. Rentschler led the work parties which, beginning in 1926, originally established the A.T. between the Lehigh and Susquehanna Rivers. Trail continues on woods road.

0.4   Leave woods road, turning right onto trail.

0.6   Cross Game Lands road which comes uphill from right. Parking lot is located 0.2 mi. to the right adjacent to PA Rt. 183.

1.4   Blue-blazed trail to the right leads 200 yds. to Black Swatara **SPRING.**

2.5   Cross small stream.

4.0   Leave obscure Game Lands road, and enter woods to the left.

4.2   Reach junction of A.T., Eagles Nest, and Little Creek Trails, Continue ahead.

5.3   Cross Sand Spring Trail. Sand **SPRING,** a fine walled spring is located 200 yds. to the right. **No camping** at or near the spring.

5.9   Cross Game Commission Administrative Road.

6.1   Cross Game Lands boundary. Enter Weiser State Forest.

6.2   Blue-blazed trail leads left 0.3 mi. to Eagle Nest **SHELTER** and Yeich **SPRING.**

8.1   Meet old cross mountain road. To the right in 1.6 mi. is Game Lands parking lot and Shartlesville, 2.0 mi. further.

SECTION 5

8.5 Bear left on old A.T.

9.0 Turn sharp right and start ascent of ridge on rock steps.

9.4 Just beyond the top of the ridge, come to Game Lands road. Cross directly, following arrows, cairns, and blazes for about 100 yds. Enter woods on trail now south of road. Footway becomes rocky.

10.2 Pass Phillip's Canyon **SPRING** Trail to the right. Spring is 135 yds. on left after a steep descent. **Variable.**

11.4 Come to Game Lands road. Cross diagonally following arrows, cairns and blazes for about 120 yds. Enter woods on trail, now north of road.

11.6 Cross Marshalls Path, a well worn, blue-blazed trail from Bellmans Gap, going right to hard-surfaced Mountain Road at foot of ridge.

12.5 Reach Auburn Lookout, a rock outcrop to the left, off trail. Excellent view of the village and surrounding area.

12.6 Come to Game Lands road. Follow road for about 45 yds. Do not cross. Re-enter woods.

12.8 Cross Game Lands road.

13.4 Come to Dynamite Road, a blue-blazed trail leading on right to Mountain Road at the foot of the ridge. Trail turns sharp left here.

13.5 Cross new pipeline.

13.9 Cross old pipeline. Shortly after, start descent of ridge, gradually at first, then steeply switching back on path which becomes a road.

14.7 Come to old railroad bed. Turn left for 45 yds., then descend bank on right via path to rail tracks. Cross these to cinder road and turn left.

15.0 Reach railroad bridge over Schuylkill River, and turn right on Broad St. in Port Clinton. Parking is limited in the village; use area on side road east of PA Rt. 61, 0.5 mi. south of the village.

Secton 6

PA RT. 183 TO SWATARA GAP

DISTANCE   18.2 Miles

This section of the trail is maintained by the Blue Mountain Eagle Climbing Club.

GENERAL INFORMATION

Road Approaches

At some highways the A.T. is marked by an official signboard erected by the Pennsylvania Department of Transportation.

Road approaches to the trail are as follows:

0.0 mi. at PA Rt. 183 the trail crosses between Strausstown and Summit Station. There is a Game Commission parking lot 0.3 mi. south of the mountaintop on the east side of the road.

6.9 mi. from PA Rt. 183. Access is by PA Rt. 501 between Bethel and Pine Grove. There is parking room just north of the crossing.

18.2 mi. from PA Rt. 183, in Swatara Gap, access is by Legislative Route (L.R.) 140, just south of the Interstate 81 overpass. No access from Interstate 81. L.R. 140 goes north from the village of Lickdale at the intersection where PA Rt. 72 turns. Limited parking.

Maps

Use KTA Section Six Map which shows much trail data, and is based upon the following USGS 7 1/2" quads: Friedensburg, Swatara Hill, Pine Grove, Fredericksburg, Indiantown Gap.

Shelters

There are no shelters in this section.

Public Accommodations

There is a hostel near Rt. 501.

SECTION 6

Supplies

The Woods Creek store and restaurant is located 0.8 mi. south of A.T. in Swatara Gap along L.R. 140. Hikers welcome.

General Description of the Trail

Except for a slight dip in Shuberts Gap, the trail stays on the ridge until the final descent into Swatara Gap. Points of interest along the way are the remains of old Fort Dietrich Snyder (1756), one of a chain of forts and blockhouses built as protection from the Indians; Showers Steps, 500 rough stone steps forming a path down the point of Round Head, built by Lloyd Showers; and Pilger Ruh Spring, a colonial watering stop.

Section 6

PA RT.183 TO SWATARA GAP

NORTH TO SOUTH

Miles Detailed Trail Data

0.0 At the official PennDOT signboard, cross the highway to the west side; go up a slight bank and follow signs and blazes across large open field on an old road leading to the former Shuberts Summit cross-mountain road. Watch for a minor relocation in this area.

0.3 Turn sharp right and in 100 yds. reach historical marker for Fort Dietrich Snyder. (See chapter on history.)

0.4 A.T. turns sharp left at marker. Blue-blazed trail ahead leads to a **SPRING** in .2 mi. which can be reached by going north on the cross-mountain road for 300 yds. Turn left across a clearing to reach spring in the woods.

3.0 Cross oil pipeline.

3.4 Arrive at Shuberts Gap. A blue-blazed trail ahead leads downhill to a dam. The water is very cold. Below the dam is private property. Do not trespass.

SECTION 6

3.5 Brook and **SPRINGS** at the Hertlein **CAMPSITE**. Cross brook.

3.6 Blue-blazed trail to the left leads 0.4 mi. to Shikellamy Summit, a fine lookout.

5.0 Turn sharp right downhill. A blue-blazed trail to the left leads to the Shanaman Marker and then to Round Head and Showers Steps, worthwhile side trip. William F. Shanaman, who was mayor of Reading, PA, was an early trailworker. Round Head is a great viewpoint. Lloyd Showers, another early trailworker, constructed a path of 500 rough stone steps down the face of Round Head. This path continues through the Kessel (kettle) and rejoins the A.T. At the base of Showers Steps is a **SPRING.**

5.3 Trail bears left below the rim of the Kessel. A relocation is scheduled for this area in order to avoid a housing development. Watch for signs.

6.6 Blue-blazed trail to the left leads to Pilger Ruh (Pilgrims Rest) **SPRING,** a watering stop dating back to colonial times. **CAMPING** is permitted a short distance to the right of the junction of the A.T. and the side trail. Watch for signs to **HOSTEL,** 0.1 mi. off the trail.

6.9 Reach PA Rt 501. Cross highway directly and descend to Kimmel Lookout, an outstanding viewpoint named for Richard Kimmel, a trailworker for over 40 years, and an honorary member of ATC.

7.2 Cross buried cable line clearing; turn left and then right along edge of mountain.

8.5 Reach PA Rt.645 at site of radio tower. Cross highway directly and enter woods. Trail becomes rocky.

9.1 Trail reaches ridge top and turns left onto an old stage road.

9.7 Reach clearing. Continue ahead on old road entering Game Lands.

10.7 Blue-blazed trail to the right leads past a register box and on to Blue Mountain **SPRING,** 200 yds. downhill.

SECTION 6

- **12.1** Cross abandoned oil pipeline. A tri-county marker, denoting the intersection of Berks, Lebanon, and Schuylkill counties is 200 yds. to the left along the pipeline.

- **12.2** Turn left from road onto a footpath.

- **13.5** Turn left onto obscure abandoned power line. Then turn right in 20 yds.

- **14.9** Dip into hollow passing the old charcoal road leading downhill to the left into Monroe Valley.

- **16.0** The white-blazed Game Lands boundary and the A.T. run together at this point. **Use caution.**

- **16.1** Leave Game Lands boundary and cross a rocky area.

- **16.9** After descending gradually on the point of the ridge, make a sharp right and begin descending the mountain on the north side.

- **17.0** Cross a charcoal hearth.

- **17.2** Trail turns left.

- **17.6** Cross woods road.

- **17.8** Approaching the fence along Interstate 81, turn left; follow blazes along and near fence. Do not cross the fence. Look for **SPRING.**

- **17.9** Turn right, passing under I-81 bridges.

- **18.0** Turn right onto hard road along the Swatara Creek.

- **18.1** Turn left and cross Swatara Creek on "Waterville Bridge," an historic iron bridge.

- **18.2** Reach L.R. 140. A.T. crosses highway.

Section 6

SWATARA GAP TO PA RT. 183

SOUTH TO NORTH

Miles   **Detailed Trail Data**

0.0   Cross PA L.R. 140; turn right along Swatara Creek.

0.1   Turn left, crossing Swatara Creek on "Waterville Bridge," an historic iron bridge.

0.2   Turn sharp left uphill under Interstate 81 bridges. Turn left, then keep the right of the fence in the woods. Look for **SPRING.**

0.4   Turn right away from fence.

0.6   Cross woods road. Trail now ascending.

1.0   Trail turns right onto woods road.

1.2   Cross circle of old charcoal hearth.

1.3   Reach crest of mountain. Trail turns left.

2.2   Use caution as confusing white Game Lands boundary blazes run with the A.T. Blazes.

3.3   Trail to the right leads down to Monroe Valley.

4.7   Reach obsure abandoned power line cut. Trail turns left and then right.

5.5   Turn right onto path.

5.9   Turn right onto woods road.

6.1   Cross oil pipeline, continuing on old stage road. To the right in 200 yds. is a tri-county marker denoting the intersection of Berks, Lebanon and Schuylkill Counties.

7.5   Blue-blazed trail leads left past a register box and in 200 yds. to Blue Mountain **SPRING.**

SECTION 6

- **8.5** Cross clearing and continue on woods road, leaving Game Lands.

- **9.0** Trail turns right into woods, descending slightly and paralleling ridge top.

- **9.7** Cross PA Rt. 645 between Fredericksburg and Pine Grove. Pass tower. Trail continues along ridge.

- **11.0** Trail turns left, then right, crossing buried cable line and descending to Kimmel Lookout. This lookout is named for Dick Kimmel, a trail worker for more than 40 years, and now an honorary member of the ATC.

- **11.3** Reach PA Rt. 501 and cross highway directly. Watch for signs to hostel, 0.1 mi. off the trail.

- **11.6** Blue-blazed trail to the right leads to Pilger Ruh (Pilgrims Rest) **SPRING,** a watering stop dating from colonial times. **CAMPING** is permitted a short distance to the left of the junction of the side trail and the A.T.

- **12.2** Bear left skirting the rim of the Kessel (kettle).

- **13.2** A.T. turns left. Blue-blazed trail to the right leads past the Shanaman Marker to Round Head and Showers steps. Excellent views. Showers Steps, 500 rough stone steps, descend the point of Round Head on the blue-blazed trail, which then circles back to rejoin the A.T. A **SPRING** is at the foot of the steps.

- **14.6** Blue-blazed trail to the right leads 0.4 mi. to Shikellamy Summit, a fine lookout.

- **14.7** Cross brook and reach the **SPRINGS** at the Hertlein **CAMPSITE.**

- **14.8** Shuberts Gap. A blue-blazed trail leads downhill to a dam. Water is very cold. Below the dam is private property. Do not trespass.

- **15.2** Cross oil pipeline.

17.8 Reach Shuberts Summit abandoned cross-mountain road. A.T. turns right for 100 yds., then left onto a woods road. A marker indicates the site of Fort Dietrich Snyder (1756), one of a chain of forts erected as protection against Indian Raids. A blue-blazed trail to the left leads 0.2 mi. to a **SPRING.** Be alert for a minor relocation in this area.

18.2 Reach PA Rt.183. To continue on the A.T., cross highway and follow woods road.

Section 7

SWATARA GAP TO CLARKS VALLEY

DISTANCE   16.9 Miles

This section of the trail is maintained by the Blue Mountain Eagle Climbing Club from Swatara Gap to Rausch Gap, and by the Brandywine Valley Outing Club from Rausch Gap to Clarks Valley.

GENERAL INFORMATION

Road Approaches

At some highways the A.T. is marked by an official signboard erected by the Pennsylvania Department of Transportation.

Road approaches to the trail are as follows:

0.0 mi., in Swatara Gap, access is by Legislative Route (L.R.) 140 just south of the Interstate 81 overpass. Limited parking. No access from Interstate 81. L.R. 140 comes north from the village of Lickdale at the intersection where PA Rt. 72 turns. There is limited parking along these roads. A new State Park is planned for this area and when construction begins parking areas may be designated by signs. Parking may be arranged at the Bashore Boy Scout Reservation, 0.9 mi. west of the A.T. on PA Rt. 443, by advance permission of the Camp Director, 630 Janet Ave., Lancaster, PA 17601.

16.9 mi. from Swatara Gap, where the A.T. crosses PA Rt 325 in Clarks Valley, there is a Game Commission parking lot. This trail crossing is located 10.1 mi. east of the intersection of PA Rt. 325 and PA Rt. 225, 2.0 mi. north of the village of Dauphin.

Maps

Use KTA Section Seven map, which shows much trail data, and is based upon the following USGS 7 1/2" quads: Indiantown Gap, Tower City, Grantville, Enders.

SECTION 7
Shelters

5.7 mi. from Swatara Gap, in Rausch Gap, the Rausch Gap Shelter has a reliable spring and outhouse facilities. This shelter was built in 1972 by the Blue Mountain Eagle Climbing Club with the permission of the PA Game Commission. No camping or fires are permitted elsewhere except as authorized. This shelter is for the use of through hikers only. The area is patrolled by Game Commission Officers, who enforce all regulations.

Public Accommodations

The Bashore Boy Scout Reservation may be used by hiking groups if advance arrangements are made with the Camp Director, Camp Bashore, Lancaster-Lebanon Boy Scout Council Office, 630 Janet Ave., Lancaster, PA 17601. Construction for through-hiker hostel "Bleu Blaze" (2.6 mi. from Swatara Gap) is under way and should be completed by summer of 1989. For information, phone (717) 397-0851 at that time.

Supplies

There is a grocery store and seasonal hamburger stand 0.7 mi. south of the A.T. in Swatara Gap. At 1.8 mi. from Swatara Gap directly on the trail in the village of Green Point is Larry's Green Point Country Store, which stocks food and supplies for hikers. There is a phone booth in front of the store.

General Description of the Trail

The first three miles of trail follow public roads, a condition which will change upon construction of a new State Park in Swatara Gap and the surrounding area. While this construction is in progress the trail may be temporarily relocated. Watch for blazes. After leaving the roads, the trail climbs Second Mountain, then descends into Stony Creek Valley and enters St. Anthony's Wilderness, the largest roadless tract in southeastern Pennsylvania. Historic Rausch Gap village is directly on the trail. An exploration of the area will reveal building foundations, a cemetary, old hand dug wells, abandoned railroad beds, railroad facilities, and other remains of a once thriving industrial community. (See the chapter on history.) The trail goes through Rausch Gap, then ascends Sharp Mountain and Stony Mountain before dropping into Clarks Valley. In addition to Rausch Gap Village and Yellow Springs Village (a long abandoned coal mining community), a point of interest is the northern terminus of the

Horse-Shoe Trail on the top of Sharp Mountain. During times when the trees are not in leaf it is possible from Stony Mountain to see DeHart Dam and the Harrisburg Water Supply Reservoir.

Section 7

SWATARA GAP TO CLARKS VALLEY

NORTH TO SOUTH

Miles   Detailed Trail Data

0.0   From west side of PA L.R. 140 pass **SPRING** and begin gradual uphill.

0.6   Reach open field; turn left.

1.0   Reach PA Rt. 433; turn left.

1.5   Pass road on right.

1.8   Pass grocery on your right.

2.0   Turn right onto a macadam road.

2.4   Bear right onto a dirt road leading into a housing development. Stay on road.

2.5   Cross small stream. Dam on right.

2.6   Turn left onto a woods road between two houses. Stay on trail. Do not trespass. (Blue-blazes to the right lead in 600 ft. to a future hostel. See "Public Accommodations," this section.)

2.9   Enter PA Game Lands. No camping or fires are permitted except as authorized. (See section on Game Lands.)

3.1   Pass a woods road on left.

3.2   Turn left uphill. A **SPRING** beside the trail may be dry in late summer.

3.7   Reach the crest of Second Mountain. Turn left and begin a gradual descent on the old wagon road.

SECTION 7

- **4.5** Cross Haystack Creek on a wooden footbridge.

- **4.7** Reach the center of the old Rausch Gap Village. Community well is on the left of the square. Do not build fires or camp here in violation of Game Commission regulations. A.T. bears right.

- **4.9** Reach the old railroad bed of the Susquehanna and Schuylkill Railroad, now a Game Commission administrative road. About 150 ft. to the right is the remains of the turntable pit. Across the road from the pit stood the passenger station. To the right the maintenance road leads 3.8 mi. to Gold Mine Road and a Game Commission parking lot. To the left the road leads to the abandoned railroad station at Cold Spring; 4.5 mi. to the site of the former Yellow Springs Station; and 14.0 mi. to Ellendale Forge and another Game Commission parking lot. The A.T. turns left here, crossing Rausch Creek on the old stone-arch railroad bridge.

- **5.1** Turn right and enter old mine road. Use care in following blazes through old mining area.

- **5.7** Blue-blazed trail to the left leads to Rausch Gap **SHELTER** and **SPRING.**

- **5.9** Pass old open-cut strip mine on left, with Rausch Creek on right shortly after trail turns toward the left. The trail will now follow an old stage road for the next 6.8 mi.

- **8.0** Bear right on old stage road at the norther terminus of the Horse-Shoe Trail. The Horse-Shoe Trail leads left downhill 0.9 mi. to the Cold Spring Station. Trail now descends slightly and in 0.2 mi. bears to the left.

- **10.3** Pass through ruins of old Yellow Springs Village. Trail continues straight through the village, then along a creek bed before crossing a narrow ravine at the remains of the old inclined plane of the mining era. Plane leads downhill 0.9 mi. to site of former Yellow Springs Station.

- **10.5** Turn right along another old stage road, now overgrown.

- **10.6** Proceed uphill on old stage road.

- **12.9** Turn sharp right off stage road onto a woods trail. The stage road continues straight ahead, descending to the abandoned village of Rattling Run.

13.0 Cross Rattling Run on stepping stones.

13.6 Reach the summit of Stony Mountain and the site of a dismantled fire tower. The trail descends to Clarks Valley on the old fire tower road.

16.6 Turn right where fire tower road levels off at the bottom of the mountain.

16.8 Cross Clarks Creek.

16.9 Reach the Game Commission parking lot and PA Rt. 325.

Section 7

CLARKS VALLEY TO SWATARA GAP

SOUTH TO NORTH

Miles   Detailed Trail Data

0.0 From PA Rt. 325 trail crosses the Game Commission parking area and onto a woods road.

0.1 Cross Clarks Creek.

0.3 Woods road turns left, beginning ascent of Stony Mountain on the old fire tower road.

3.3 Reach the summit of Stony Mountain and the site of dismantled fire tower. A.T. becomes a woods trail.

3.9 Cross rattling Run.

4.0 A.T. turns left onto an old stage road, which the trail follows for 6.8 mi.

6.4 Trail turns left, crossing a narrow ravine at the remains of an old inclined plane which descended to the railroad in the valley at the former Yellow Springs Station. Trail continues uphill along a creek bed.

6.6 Pass through the ruins of Yellow Springs Village.

SECTION 7

- **8.9** Pass through a small clearing at the northern terminus of the Horse-Shoe Trail, which descends to the right to the old Cold Spring Staton and the ruins of a former resort. A.T. bears left.

- **11.0** Trail turns right, leaving the old stage road. Pass a large open-cut strip mine on the right, with Rausch Creek on the left.

- **11.2** Blue-blazed trail to the right leads to the Rausch Gap **SHELTER** and **SPRING**.

- **11.8** Trail turns left onto the cinder administrative road of the Game Commission. This road is the former road bed of the Susquehanna and Schuylkill Railroad, which ceased operations in the 1940's.

- **12.0** Cross Rausch Creek on an old stone arch railroad bridge. Directly after crossing the creek, turn right onto a woods road. The Game Commission road continues 3.8 mi. to the Gold Mine Road and Game Commission parking lot. An old turntable pit is 150 ft. ahead to the right of the road. Across the road from the turntable pit is the site of the old Rausch Gap station.

- **12.1** Pass through the ruins of the old Rausch Gap Village. No camping or fires permitted except as authorized.

- **12.3** Trail bears right where road forks.

- **12.4** Cross Haystack Creek and begin ascending Second Mountain.

- **13.2** Reach the crest of Second Mountain and turn right, descending.

- **13.6** Pass **SPRING** on left of trail and then turn right on old woods road.

- **13.7** Pass road coming in from right.

- **13.9** Leave PA Game Lands and enter private property.

- **14.2** Turn right onto a well used road. Descend hill; cross small stream. Stay on road. (Blue-blazes lead straight ahead 600 ft. to future hostel. See "Public Accommodations," this section.)

- **14.4** Turn left onto a macadam road.

14.9	Turn left onto PA Rt. 443, passing grocery on left, which caters to hikers.
15.4	Pass road on the left. A new State Park will be constructed in the Swatara Gap area. During the construction of the dam and new highways, the Trail may be temporarily relocated from time to time. Use caution and be alert for changes.
15.9	Turn right, leaving PA Rt. 443 and going along fence row in open field.
16.3	Turn right, entering woods. Start gradual uphill.
16.9	Reach PA L.R. 140, passing **SPRING.**

Section 8

CLARKS VALLEY TO SUSQUEHANNA RIVER

DISTANCE   17.0 Miles

This section of the trail is maintained from Clarks Valley to PA Rt. 225 by the Susquehanna Appalachian Trail Club, and from PA Rt. 225 to the Susquehanna River by the York Hiking Club.

GENERAL INFORMATION

Road Approaches

At some highways the A.T. is marked by an official signboard erected by the Pennsylvania Department of Transportation.

Road approaches to the trail are as follows:

0.0 mi., in Clarks Valley, the A.T. crosses PA Rt. 325 10.1 mi. east of the intersection of PA Rt. 325 and PA Rt. 225. This intersection is 2.0 mi. north of the Village of Dauphin. A Game Lands parking lot is located at the trail crossing.

9.2 mi., from Clarks Valley, the A.T. crosses PA Rt. 225 at the crest of Peters Mountain. Parking on east side of highway.

16.3 mi. from Clarks Valley, the A.T. crosses U.S. Rts. 22 and 322 at the east end of the Clarks Ferry Bridge. Adequate parking along the river, adjacent to the highway.

17.0 mi. from Clarks Valley, at the west end of the Clarks Ferry Bridge along U.S. Rts. 22 and 322, is limited parking.

Maps

Use KTA Section Eight Map which shows much trail data, and is based upon the following USGS 7½" quads: Enders, Halifax, Duncannon.

Shelters

6.1 mi. from Clarks Valley is the Peters Mountain Shelter. Spring is located 275 yds. down a steep blue-blazed trail on the north side of the mountain.

7.6 mi. from Clarks Valley is the Zeager Shelter. No water.

13.5 mi. from Clarks Valley is the Clarks Ferry Shelter. Good spring.

Public Accommodations

There are no public accommodations on this section of the trail. Just beyond the west end of the Clarks Ferry Bridge, in the Village of Amity Hall, are two motels and a restaurant. The town of Duncannon, through which the trail passes, is 0.6 mi. south of this section. Duncannon offers lodging and restaurants.

Supplies

There are no opportunities to purchase supplies on this section of the trail. Supplies may be purchased in Duncannon.

General Description of the Trail

After the initial steep climb to the crest of Peters Mountain, the trail stays on the ridge top with only minor changes in elevation until the descent to the Susquehanna River. This descent is gradual at first, but then becomes steeper, making use of switchbacks to reach the railroad and the highway beyond. Points of interest along the trail include Shikellimy Rocks, Table Rock, and excellent views up and down the Susquehanna River. The Juniata River can be seen to the north, and to the south is the Rockville Bridge, the longest stone arch railroad bridge in the world. This bridge, built in 1902, carries Conrail's mainline tracks across the Susquehanna River.

Section 8

CLARKS VALLEY TO SUSQUEHANNA RIVER

NORTH TO SOUTH

Miles   Detailed Trail Data

0.0   Cross PA Rt. 325, entering the woods in PA Game Lands, and begin ascent of Peters Mountain.

0.4 Blue-blazed trail to the left leads 100 yds. to a **SPRING.**

0.8 Reach the crest of the mountain. Trail turns left along the crest.

1.4 Reach bottom of the small gap. Continue along ridge top.

2.1 Blue-blazed Shikellimy Trail to the left leads down the mountain 1.0 mi. to PA Rt. 325, thence right along the highway, past a small **SPRING** in the woods 90 yds. to the right, to YMCA Camp Shikellimy. A.T. continues along ridge.

2.8 Bear left, climbing Shikellimy Rocks overlooking the valley.

3.5 Blue-blazed trail to the left leads to viewpoint in 30 yds.

5.3 Bear left on an abandoned cross-mountain road. This road leads right to Powells Valley an the village of Enterline.

5.4 A.T. turns right up the mountain. Blue-blazed Victoria Trail leads 1.5 mi. to PA Rt. 325 and the site of the Victoria Furnace, a Revolutionary War era iron furnace.

6.1 Reach the Peters Mountain **SHELTER** on your left. No bunks. Water is found at a **SPRING** located 275 yds. down a blue-blazed trail on the north side of the mountain. Water is difficult to obtain at this site.

7.0 Yellow-blazed trail to the right leads in 1.5 mi. to Camp Hebron, a church camp.

7.1 Table Rock, 15 yds. to the left, with a good view.

7.3 Pass over Fumitory Rocks.

7.6 Reach the Zeager **SHELTER** on your left. Bunks for six. No water.

8.5 Pass under double power lines with excellent views at the crest.

9.0 Pass a radio facility of the Pennsylvania Department of Environmental Resources on your left.

9.2 Reach parking area, then cross PA Rt. 225 diagonally downhill to the left, and in 45 yds. turn right up a steep bank.

SECTION 8

- **9.5** Reach access road to a microwave tower.

- **9.6** Leave the access road to the right and follow the crest of the mountain to the tower.

- **10.1** Pass to the right of the Bell Telephone relay tower. A.T. then crosses a pipeline right-of-way before entering the woods and continuing straight along the ridge.

- **12.1** Cross another pipeline with good views south to Dauphin Gap, Rockville Bridge, and the city of Harrisburg.

- **12.5** Pass a rock overhang which could be used as an emergency shelter.

- **13.1** Cross under the power line. From the crest there are excellent views of the Rockville Bridge to the south and the Juniata and Susquehanna Rivers to the north. (Watch for rattlesnakes at the viewpoint.) After leaving the power line clearing continue along the very rocky ridgetop before descending onto a bench on the south face of the mountain.

- **13.5** Blue-blazed side trail to the left leads 300 ft. to the new Clarks Ferry **SHELTER**, and 600 ft. to a reliable piped **SPRING**.

- **13.9** After passing through a grove of mountain laurel, the trail reaches the crest of the mountain.

- **14.6** Power line with excellent views.

- **15.0** The trail follows the crest to the west over rock outcroppings and through wooded areas to the point of the mountain.

- **15.5** The trail descends by large switchbacks to a good view of Sherman's Creek across the Susquehanna River.

- **15.6** Reach a logging road and follow it a short distance; turn left and descend a short distance more before turning right through a brief wooded area. Cross another logging road, a logged area, and an intermittent stream to an old stone foundation, 150 ft. to the right. This is the remains of a mule barn used for logging at the turn of the century.

- **16.1** The trail descends by switchbacks for 0.25 mi. to the railroad.

16.3 After crossing the tracks, the trail turns right to the Appalachian Trail sign at the east end of the Clarks Ferry Bridge. Turn left and cross the highway with care.

17.0 Reach the west end of the bridge.

Section 8

SUSQUEHANNA RIVER TO CLARKS VALLEY

SOUTH TO NORTH

Miles   Detailed Trail Data

0.0 Begin section at the west end of the Clarks Ferry Bridge. Cross the bridge on the pedestrian walkway.

0.4 At the east end of the bridge cross the highway. Turn right at the Appalachian Trail sign and follow the highway and railroad for 0.25 mi.

0.7 The trail turns left and crosses the railroad. Then ascend by switchbacks for 0.2 mi. to a bench.

0.9 The trail levels and follows the bench edge to the southwest.

1.2 About 150 ft. to the left is an old stone foundation for a mule barn dating to the turn of the century when it was used in connection with lumbering operations. Shortly after passing the foundation, the trail crosses an intermittent stream, a logging area, and a logging road. After passing briefly through a wooded area, the trail bears left up the mountain.

1.4 Reach another woods road. Turn right and follow the road to the end. The trail continues up to the end of the mountain where there is a good view of Sherman's Creek across the river.

1.5 The trail switches back at the viewpoint and continues climbing to the crest of the mountain by large switchbacks to rock outcroppings at the top, which offer good views to the north and south.

2.0 The trail follows the crest to the east through wooded areas and over rock outcroppings.

SECTION 8

2.4 Power line with excellent views.

3.1 The trail leaves the crest to a bench on the south face of the mountain, passing through some mountain laurel.

3.5 Blue-blazed side trail leads 300 ft. to the new Clarks Ferry **SHELTER,** and 600 ft. to a reliable **SPRING.**

3.9 The trail regains the mountain crest after passing the side trail. It then goes over large rocks before crossing under the power line. From the crest there are excellent views of the Rockville Bridge to the south, and of the Juniata and Susquehanna Rivers to the north. (Watch for rattlesnakes at this viewpoint.) The trail now follows an old woods road for about 400 yds.

4.5 Pass a rock overhang which could be used as an emergency shelter.

4.9 Cross a pipeline with good views south to Dauphin Gap, the Rockville Bridge, and Harrisburg City.

6.9 The A.T. leaves the woods and crosses another pipeline right-of-way before passing to the left of the Bell Telephone relay tower. The trail re-enters the woods and continues along the ridge.

7.4 Reach the access road for the microwave tower and turn left.

7.5 The trail leaves the access road to the left.

7.8 Reach PA Rt. 225, crossing the road uphill; then bear right on a dirt road leading to trailhead parking area.

8.0 Pass a radio facility of the Pennsylvania Department of Environmental Resources on the right.

8.5 Pass under power line with excellent views at the crest.

9.4 Arrive at the Zeager **SHELTER** on the right. No water.

9.7	Pass over Fumitory Rocks.
9.9	Table Rock with good views is 15 yds. to the right.
10.0	Side trail with yellow blazes leads to the left, reaching Camp Hebron (church camp) in 1.5 mi.
10.9	Arrive at the Peters Mountin **SHELTER**. No bunks. **SPRING** is 275 yds. down a blue-blazed trail on the north side of the mountain. Water is difficult to obtain at this site.
11.5	Blue-blazed Victoria Trail leads downhill to the right, reaching Pa. Rt. 325 in 1.5 mi. To the left, this cross-mountain road leads to Powells Valley and the Village of Enterline.
13.5	Blue-blazed trail to the right leads to viewpoint in 30 yds.
14.2	Trail bears right and climbs onto Shikellimy Rocks with good views of the valley.
14.9	Blue-blazed Shikellimy Trail leads right 1.0 mi. to Pa. 325, then right along the highway past a small **SPRING** (90 yds. in the woods) to Camp Shikellimy, a YMCA Camp.
15.6	Trail drops into a small gap, then ascends ridge.
16.2	A.T. turns sharp right descending Peters Mountain.
16.6	Blue-blazed trail to the right leads 100 yds. to a **SPRING.**
17.0	Reach Pa. 325. Across the highway is a large Game Lands parking area. This is the end of this section.

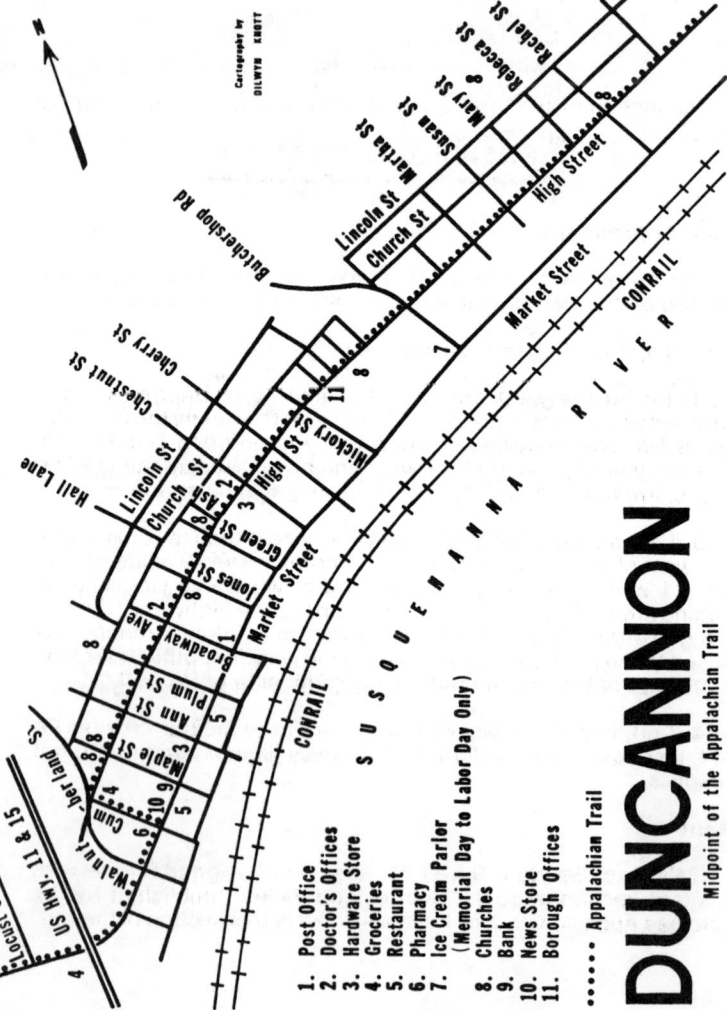

Section 9

SUSQUEHANNA RIVER TO PA 944

DISTANCE   14.7 Miles

This section of the Trail is maintained by the Mountain Club of Maryland.

GENERAL INFORMATION

Road Approaches

At some highways the A.T. is marked by an official signboard erected by the Pennsylvania Department of Transportation.

Road approaches to the Trail are as follows:

0.0 mi. at the west end of the Clarks Ferry Bridge over the Susquehanna River, along U.S. 22-322, the Trail takes the first road to the left, crossing the Juniata River, and entering Duncannon. There is limited parking at the west end of the Susquehanna River bridge. Parking is available on the streets of Duncannon.

10.6 mi. from the Susquehanna River, where the Trail crosses PA 850 west of the Village of Keystone (approximately 9 miles west of U.S. 11 and 15 at Marysville) there are two Game Commission parking areas. One is located 0.4 mi. north of the highway at the end of a gravel road which the Trail utilizes. This parking area may be closed to the public at certain times of the year. The other is located .4 mi. east of the gravel road on the south side of PA 850.

14.7 mi. from the Susquehanna River where the trail crosses PA 944, just east of Donnellytown, Extremely limited parking. Do not trespass.

Maps

KTA's map "Sections 9 and 10" has been designed for use with this trail section. Map 1, "Cumberland Valley", published by the Potomac Appalachian Trail Club, also covers this section of the trail.

SECTION 9

Shelters

5.6 mi. from the Susquehanna River is the Thelma Marks Memorial Shelter, built in 1960. An intermittent spring is 400 ft. downhill on a blue-blazed trail.

12.8 mi. from the Susquehanna River is the Darlington Shelter constructed in the spring of 1977, by the Mountain Club of Maryland.

Public Accommodations

Just beyond the west end of the Clarks Ferry Bridge in the Village of Amity Hall, are motels and a restaurant. Duncannon offers lodging, restaurants, a laundromat, a pharmacy, and other places of business, which hikers will find accommodating. Map immediately preceding this section shows location of these services.

Supplies

Supplies may be purchased in Duncannon at a number of stores.

Duncannon

The Borough of Duncannon takes special pride in its claim to be the approximate midpoint of the Appalachian Trail. Of course, the exact midpoint changes with each relocation, but it seems likely that of towns through which the Trail passes, Duncannon is probably the one nearest to the Trail's center. Consequently a special community effort is made to accommodate hikers. The Borough has posted a hiker facility map at either end of town, and a reproduction of this map is included in this Guide immediately preceding this section.

General Description of the Trail

From the west end of the Clarks Ferry Bridge the first two miles are on paved roads through the town of Duncannon. A steep climb up Cove Mountain ends at Hawk Rock with outstanding views. The Trail then keeps on the ridge, through the woods with footing rocky, then descending to cross PA Rt. 850, followed by the climb and descent of Little Mountain and the climb and descent of Blue Mountain before reaching PA Hwy. 944. Points of interest are Hawk Rock and the Darlington Shelter, a prefabricated shelter with no piece weighing more than 80 pounds. At the crest of Blue Mountain, the Trail shares the ridge with the Tuscarora Trail, blazed orange. Deans Gap is a junction of three trails: the Appalachian Trail, the Tuscarora Trail, and the Darlington Trail.

Section 9

SUSQUEHANNA RIVER TO PA 944

NORTH TO SOUTH

Miles   Detailed Trail Data

0.0   From the west end of the Clarks Ferry Bridge take the first road to the left, crossing over the Juniata River and then crossing under railroad tracks. Turn right for 1 block on PA 849 (Newport Road), then turn left onto High Street.

1.7   Turn left onto Cumberland Street, then right onto Market Street, crossing the Little Juniata Creek. Cross under Routes 11 and 15 and then turn left on the old road passing several places of business.

2.1   Cross the Shermans Creek bridge and continue on paved road for 0.2 miles. Trail turns sharply to the right across the road from the old motel and bar. Trail ascends steeply onto the flank of Cove Mountain and in 0.5 miles joins an old mountain road ascending the north side of the ridge.

3.5   Cross a rock slide. Trail becomes a footpath.

3.8   Reach Hawk Rock with fine views of the rivers and of Peters Mountain.

5.6   Blue-blazed trail to the left leads 500 feet to the Thelma Marks Memorial **SHELTER**. Intermittent **SPRING** is 400 ft. further down the mountain on a blue-blazed trail.

6.6   Blue-blazed trail to the right leads down the mountain to the service road of the Duncannon Water Company.

8.2   Cross pipeline clearing on Cove Mtn. (Fine views)

8.8   Begin descent of mountain.

9.3   Cross stream.

9.4   A.T. turns left onto woods road.

9.7   Trail turns right onto another woods road.

SECTION 9

- **10.0** A.T. turns left and follows new relocation through woods and field.

- **10.6** Reach PA 850, A.T. turns right and follows paved road.

- **10.8** Reach official PennDot A.T. signboard at the junction of PA 850 with Millers Gap Road. A.T. turns left onto Millers Gap Road.

- **11.0** Turn right and cross farm field.

- **11.1** Turn left into wooded ravine.

- **11.5** Reach telephone cable clearing. Trail turns left, follows along clearing and ascends Little Mountain.

- **11.7** A.T. turns right into woods.

- **11.9** After descending Little Mountain, trail turns right onto woods road.

- **12.5** A.T. turns left and begins ascent of Blue Mountain.

- **12.8** Reach top of mountain. Blue-blazed trail on left leads to the Darlington **SHELTER** and **SPRING**. Shelter is approximately 200 yds. and spring is approximately 0.25 miles from A.T.

- **12.9** Cross ridgetop jeep road. Orange blazes mark the Darlington Trail, which follows the jeep road.

- **13.3** Reach rock outcrop, which provides a good overlook across the valley. Trail continues to descend.

- **13.5** Turn right onto woods road. Seasonal **SPRING** to the right just beyond the turn.

- **13.6** Turn left off woods road. Trail enters partially timbered area and continues descending, more gradually.

- **13.8** Trail turns right onto dirt road.

- **14.7** Reach PA 944, just east of Donnellytown, and the end of this section. The Trail crosses the highway and continues straight ahead on Deer Lane.

Section 9

PA 944 TO SUSQUEHANNA RIVER

SOUTH TO NORTH

Miles   Detailed Trail Data

0.0   From PA 944, just east of Donnellytown, the Trail proceeds toward Blue Mountain on a dirt road.

0.9   Trail turns right into partially timbered area and begins ascent of Blue Mountain.

1.1   Turn right onto woods road.

1.2   Reach seasonal **SPRING.** Just past the spring turn left, leaving woods road and resume ascent.

1.4   Reach stone steps and rock outcrop, which provides a good overlook across the valley.

1.8   Cross ridgetop jeep road. Orange blazes mark the Darlington Trail, which follows the jeep road.

1.9   Reach blue-blazed trail on right, which leads in 200 yds. to the Darlington **SHELTER** and to a **SPRING** in approximately 0.25 miles. A.T. begins descent of the Blue Mountain.

2.2   Trail turns right onto woods road.

2.8   Trail turns left and ascends Little Mountain.

3.0   Reach telephone cable clearing. A.T. turns left and follows clearing.

3.2   Trail turns right into the woods.

3.6   Reach end of wooded ravine, turn right and cross farm field.

3.7   Reach Millers Gap Road. A.T. turns left.

3.9   Reach PA 850. From the official PennDot A.T. signboard at the junction of Millers Gap Road and PA 850, trail turns right and follows along PA 850.

SECTION 9

4.1 Trail turns left into field with blazed posts.

4.4 Enter woods

4.7 Turn right onto woods road.

5.0 Trail turns left onto woods road.

5.3 A.T. turns right onto a woods road.

5.4 Cross stream and soon begin ascent of Cove Mountain.

6.5 Cross pipeline clearing with good views.

8.0 Blue-blazed trail to the left leads down to the service road of the Duncannon Water Company.

9.0 Blue-blazed trail to the right leads 500 ft. to the Thelma Marks Memorial **SHELTER**. **SPRING** is 400 ft. further down the mountain on the blue-blazed trail.

10.8 Reach Hawk Rock with fine views of the rivers and of Peters Mountain. Begin descent of north side of Cove Mountain.

11.1 Cross a rock slide. Trail becomes an old road.

11.6 Old road becomes a trail which crosses the nose of Cove Mountain and descends to the old highway across the road from the old motel and bar. Turn sharp left following the highway for 0.2 miles to Shermans Creek bridge.

12.3 Cross bridge over Shermans Creek and continue straight ahead on the old highway passing several places of business.

12.8 Reach the junction of PA 274. Trail turns right passing under U.S. Highways 11 and 15 and continues ahead crossing the Little Juniata Creek and entering the center of Duncannon on Market Street. Trail then turns left onto Cumberland Street and right onto High Street. See special note regarding the Borough of Duncannon at the introduction to this section.

14.1 Turn right onto Newport Road, PA 849.

14.2 Turn left crossing under a railroad overpass and then crossing the bridge over the Juniata.

14.7 Reach the west end of the Clarks Ferry Bridge over the Susquehanna River. This is the end of this section. To continue on A.T. cross the bridge.

Section 10

PA 944 TO CHURCHTOWN

DISTANCE   10.7 Miles

This section of the Trail is maintained by the Mountain Club of Maryland.

GENERAL INFORMATION

Road Approaches

At some highways the A.T. is marked by an official signboard erected by the Pennsylvania Department of Transportation.

Road approaches to the trail are as follows:

This section of the Trail is unusual in that practically all of it is along or upon hard surfaced roads because of the necessity of crossing the highly developed Cumberland Valley. Parking is available at many places.

Maps

KTA's map "Sections 9 and 10" has been designed for use with this trail section. Map 1, "Cumberland Valley," published by the Potomac Appalachian Trail Club, also covers this section of the trail.

Shelters

There are no shelters in this section.

Public Accommodations

0.7 mi. east of the Trail on US 11, in the village of New Kingston, is a motel and deli.

1.0 mi. west of the Trail on US 11 are several motels and restaurants near the Interstate 81 interchange.

SECTION 10
Supplies

There are no convenient places to purchase supplies in this section. There is a store located in an old red barn building at the west end of the trailer park near Bernhisel Bridge, about 0.5 mi. from the Trail. Of course, Carlisle, which is located about 6 miles west of the Trail, offers a full range of public facilities.

Special Note

At about midpoint in the Cumberland Valley, the Musser Farm operates a vegetable stand just east of where the A.T. crosses Trindle Road, PA 641. For A.T. hikers, at a location 1 mi. south of Trindle Road, Mr. Musser will provide water, a place to pitch a tent, and toilet access, free of charge. There will be a modest charge for any other services (food, shower, shelter, etc.). The vegetable stand is CLOSED ON SUNDAYS and no facilities are available at that time. It is important not to disturb the Mussers on Sundays. The Mussers are located 4.5 mi. south of US 11; 7 mi south of Bernhisel Bridge. Since there is a long gap between shelters, this way-station is intended to assist through-hikers.

General Description of the Trail.

From PA 944 the Trail goes south on macadam and gravel roads for a short distance then into the woods along the Conodoguinet Creek. After crossing the creek, the next 10 mi. are of necessity on roads in order to cross the highly developed Cumberland Valley. The Valley is mostly residential along the route of the Trail and few commercial businesses are passed. There is little shade in the Valley and summer hiking can be hot and dry. CARRY WATER. Beware of dogs. You will be passing many homes and farms, and dogs frequently are left to run loose.

NOTE: The National Park Service is now in the process of acquiring a right-of-way to permit the trail to cross the Cumberland Valley largely on an off-road route. This effort will be continuing over the next two to three years, during which time there will be periodic relocations. Be alert and watch for these impending improvements as you cross the valley.

Section 10

PA 944 TO CHURCHTOWN

NORTH TO SOUTH

Miles   Detailed Trail Data

0.0 From PA 944 just east of Donnellytown, the Trail leads south on Deer Lane.

0.8 Turn right onto Sherwood Drive.

1.2 After an S turn in the road, bear left on a grassy lane with stone walls on each side.

1.4 Reach Conodoguinet Creek and turn right following the bank.

2.2 Climb an embankment to the road, then turn left crossing the creek on Bernhisel Bridge. Trail now generally follows Bernhisel Road.

2.4 Turn right, leaving roadside and follow sidehill path along the Conodoguinet Creek.

2.6 Return to Bernhisel Road.

3.5 Cross over Interstate 81.

4.2 Turn right onto Ridge Hill Road.

4.4 Turn right onto US 11, and in 0.5 mi. turn left onto Appalachian Drive.

5.6 Cross over Pennsylvania Turnpike.

6.4 Turn left onto Old Stone House Road.

8.3 Cross Trindle Road, PA 641.

9.6 Cross Lisburn Road, passing an official PennDot A.T. signboard, and continue on Old Stone House Road.

SECTION 10

10.7 Reach Churchtown (Allen P.O.). Cross Boiling Springs Road and continue straight ahead on Old Stone House Road, crossing York Road, Lutztown Road, and R.R. tracks until reaching Leidigh Road.

Secton 10

CHURCHTOWN TO PA 944

SOUTH TO NORTH

Miles   Detailed Trail Data

0.0 From Boiling Springs Road the Trail leads north on Old Stone House Road.

1.1 Cross Lisburn Road, passing an official PennDot A.T. Signboard, and continue on Old Stone House Road.

2.4 Cross Trindle Road, PA 641.

4.3 Turn right onto Appalachian Drive.

5.1 Cross over Pennsylvania Turnpike.

6.4 Turn right onto US 11, and in 0.5 mi. turn left onto Ridge Hill Road.

6.6 Turn left onto Bernhisel Road.

7.3 Cross over Interstate 81.

8.2 Turn left off Bernhisel Road and follow sidehill path along Conodoguinet Creek.

8.4 Return to Bernhisel Road.

8.5 After crossing the Conodoguinet Creek on Bernhisel Bridge, turn sharp right down the embankment and then left along the creek bank.

9.3 Leave the stream bank, bearing to your left.

9.4 Turn right onto a paved road, named Sherwood Drive.

9.9 Turn left onto Deer Lane.

10.7 Reach PA 944. End of this section. To continue on A.T. cross road onto a gravel road.

Section 11

CHURCHTOWN TO PA 94

DISTANCE   9.9 Miles

This section of the Trail is maintained by the Mountain Club of Maryland.

GENERAL INFORMATION

Road Approaches

At some highways the A.T. is marked by an official signboard erected by the Pennsylvania Department of Transportation.

Road approaches to the Trail are as follows:

0.0 mi. in Churchtown, there is parking on the village streets.

2.0 mi. from Churchtown, there is parking along Creek Road near the intersection with Kuhn Drive.

9.6 mi. from Churchtown, where the Trail crosses Sheet Iron Road, there is parking available by the side of the road.

9.9 mi. from Churchtown, where the Trail crosses PA 94, there is limited parking. Do not trespass.

Maps

KTA's map "Sections 11 and 12" has been designed for use with this trail section. Map 1, "Cumberland Valley," published by the Potomac Appalachian Trail Club, also covers this section of the trail.

Shelters

2.6 mi. from Churchtown there is a new Campbell Spring Shelter for 10.

Public Accommodations

There are motels and restaurants in the town of Mount Holly Springs, located 2.5 miles north of the A.T. on PA 94.

Supplies

Supplies can be purchased in the town of Mount Holly Springs.

General Description of the Trail

From Churchtown south, the first two miles are on paved roads, then beginning with the climb to White Rocks Ridge you will be in the woods for the next seven miles. This section is a series of climbs and descents with elevation changes of about 500 feet. Points of interest are several large sycamore trees, White Rocks Ridge, and Rocky Ridge where the Trail leads through a maze of rock formations.

Section 11

CHURCHTOWN TO PA 94

NORTH TO SOUTH

Miles   **Detailed Trail Data**

0.0   In the center of Churchtown where the Trail comes in from the north, continue ahead on the hard road, now known as Leidigh Road.

0.6   Cross PA 74 at a small cemetery. Note the official PennDot signboard.

0.9   Note a large sycamore tree on your left. This tree, 19 feet in circumference, may be the largest tree along the entire A.T. The trail continues ahead, crossing Lutztown Road and then passing a castle-like house.

1.6   Cross the Reading Railroad tracks, then Yellow Breeches Creek, and then turn left onto Creek Road.

2.0   Note the large sycamore at the edge of Yellow Breeches Creek. Trail continues ahead bearing right onto Kuhn Drive.

2.4   Trail turns right, into the woods. Parking for autos available along the road edge.

2.6 Pass trail to Campbell Spring **SHELTER** 40 yds. east of trail. Shelter is a one room semi-enclosed cabin opened in early 1984. Accommodates 10. Water available at Campbell **SPRING.**

2.7 Pass blue-blazed side trail leading 15 yards east to Campbell **SPRING.**

2.8 Trail turns left and climbs steeply to White Rocks Ridge.

3.0 At the top, the Trail turns right following the ridge and winding through and over an outcropping of hard quartzite rock. This ancient rock, dating back some 550 million years, forms one of the outlines of the greater South Mountain and marks the northern terminus of the Blue Ridge Mountains. The Trail is rough and rocky and slippery in wet weather.

3.3 High point with fine views.

3.8 A.T. turns left down a switchback trail. Blue-blazed Old Mine Trail comes in from the right. Blue-blazed trail straight ahead leads 0.1 mi. to Center Point Knob, the one time mid-point of the A.T.

3.9 Cross a woods road. Ascend and descend the side of Colon Hill.

4.9 Cross a trail with orange blazes, which to the left leads 1.7 mi. to Boy Scout Camp Tuckahoe. Immediately cross Little Dogwood Run and pass through an old charcoal hearth.

5.8 Cross a pipeline which looks like a narrow road, then ascend Little Rocky Ridge through the woods.

6.4 Pass a rock outcrop on the left and descend down ridge.

7.0 Pass Whiskey **SPRING** on the left, always flowing. Turn left onto Whiskey Spring Road. In 30 yards turn right uphill following the crest of Rocky Ridge through a maze of rock formations, with a good view of Cumberland Valley to the right.

7.9 Trail bears right.

8.0 Pass vista. A.T. continues on, descending rocky ridge by switchbacks.

8.3 Cross unmarked trail.

8.4 Cross Old Town Road.

8.5 Cross old road.

8.8 Cross old road, then telephone line right-of-way, then stream.

8.9 Trail bears right at junction.

9.1 Cross stream.

9.6 Cross Sheet Iron Road.

9.8 Cross under a power line.

9.9 Reach PA 94 at a point 2.5 mi. south of Mount Holly Springs.

To continue on A.T. cross highway.

Section 11

PA 94 TO CHURCHTOWN

SOUTH TO NORTH

Miles   **Detailed Trail Data**

0.0 From PA 94, the Trail enters the woods.

0.1 Cross under a power line.

0.3 Cross Sheet Iron Road.

0.8 Cross stream.

1.1 Cross stream, then telephone line right-of-way, then old road.

1.4 Cross old road.

1.5 Cross Old Town Road.

1.6 Cross unmarked trail. Trail now ascends Rocky Ridge by switchbacks.

1.9 Reach top of ridge and viewpoint. A.T. now follows the ridge crest passing through a maze of rock formations to the east end of the ridge, then descends to Whiskey Spring road.

2.8 Turn left onto Whiskey Spring Road. In 30 yds. pass Whiskey **SPRING** on the right, always running. Turn right into the woods. Ascend Little Rocky Ridge.

3.5 Pass a rock outcrop on the right, then descend ridge through the woods.

4.1 Cross a pipeline which looks like a narrow road. Ascend Murphy Hill (Cabin Hill) and descend to a charcoal hearth.

5.0 Cross Little Dogwood Run. Immediately cross a trail blazed with orange markings which to the right leads in 1.7 mi. to Boy Scout Camp Tuckahoe. Ascend and descend the side of Colon Hill. Then cross a woods road before ascending by switchback to White Rocks Ridge.

6.0 Turn right at top and follow crest. Blue-blazed trail on left leads 0.1 mi. to Center Point Knob, the one time mid-point of the A.T. Blue-blazed trail straight ahead is the Old Mine Trail which is now badly eroded and used mostly by vehicles. Trail follows the ridge, winding through and over an out-cropping of hard quartzite rock. This ancient rock, dating back some 550 million years, forms one of the outlines of the greater South Mountain and marks the northern terminus of the Blue Ridge Mountains. The trail is rough and rocky, and slippery in wet weather.

6.6 High point with fine views.

6.9 Trail turns left and descends steeply.

7.1 Trail turns right on old woods road.

7.2 Pass blue-blazed trail to Campbell **SPRING**, 15 yds. to the east. Turn left leaving woods road.

7.3 Pass side trail to Campbell Spring **SHELTER**, 40 yds. to the east. Shelter is a one room semi-enclosed cabin opened in early 1984. Accommodates 10. Water available at Campbell **SPRING.**

SECTION 11

7.5 Reach Kuhn Road. Turn left. Parking for vehicles available along the edge of the road.

7.9 Bear left onto Creek Road. Note the large sycamore tree on the right along Yellow Breeches Creek.

8.1 Turn right onto Leidigh Road and cross Yellow Breeches Creek.

8.3 Cross the railroad tracks.

8.9 Pass a castle-like house on the right, then cross Lutztown Road.

9.0 Note the large sycamore tree on your right. This tree, 19 feet in circumference, may be the largest tree on the entire A.T.

9.3 Cross PA 74 at a small cemetery. Note the official PennDot signboard.

9.9 Reach the center of Churchtown (Allen) at the intersection of Main Street and PA 174.

To continue on the A.T., cross PA 174 staying on Main Street which then becomes known as Old Stone House Road.

Section 12

PA 94 TO PINE GROVE FURNACE

DISTANCE 10.9 Miles

This section of the Trail is maintained by the Mountain Club of Maryland.

GENERAL INFORMATION

Road Approaches

At some highways the A.T. is marked by an official signboard erected by the Pennsylvania Department of Transportation.

Road approaches to the Trail are as follows:

0.0 mi. at PA 94, the Trail crosses 2.5 miles south of Mount Holly Springs. Limited parking.

2.0 mi. from PA 94, the Trail crosses PA 34. Limited parking.

2.8 mi. from PA 94, the Trail crosses Green Mountain Road. Limited parking.

10.6 mi. from PA 94, in Pine Grove Furnace State Park there is adequate parking. Check at the Park office for regulations governing the parking of vehicles.

Maps

KTA's map "Sections 11 and 12 has been designed for use with this trail section. Map 2 and 3 (combined), "Michaux State Forest, Pennsylvania," published by the Potomac Appalachian Trail Club, also covers this section of the trail.

Shelters

3.3 mi. from PA 94 is a blue-blazed trail leading 0.2 miles to the Tagg Run Shelters. There are two shelters, each with a raised sleeping platform, and each able to accommodate about five persons. A spring is 500 feet beyond the shelters. An unusual outhouse facility is at the site. These shelters were relocated to the current site by the Mountain Club of Maryland in 1976.

Public Accommodations

There are motels and restaurants in Mount Holly Springs, 2.5 miles north of the Trail from both PA 94 and PA 34. Pine Grove Furnace State Park offers campsites and swimming facilities. There is also a seasonal snack bar in the Park.

Supplies

Supplies may be purchased in Mount Holly Springs. In Pine Grove Furnace State Park there is a small store 50 yards off the Trail on the south side of PA 233. The store is seasonal and is generally open seven days a week between Memorial Day and Labor Day, although it may be open at other times. West of the Pine Grove Road crossing along Pine Grove Road are two public campgrounds. Tagg Run Campground (0.4 miles) has a small camp store and snack bar which is open year round. Mountain Creek Campground (1.4 miles) has a camp store.

General Description of the Trail

This section is generally in the woods all the way. After leaving PA 94, climb and descend Trents Hill, then ascend Piney Mountain, walking along the ridge before descending to Pine Grove Furnace State Park. Points of interest are the sheer, conspicuous quartzite cliffs of Pole Steeple, 0.5 mile off the Trail atop Piney Mountain; and the ruins of the old Pine Grove Furnace. The park office houses a small, but interesting museum of the natural and industrial history of the area.

Section 12

PA 94 TO PINE GROVE FURNACE

NORTH TO SOUTH

Miles   **Detailed Trail Data**

0.0   Enter the woods at a point 2.5 mi. south of Mount Holly Springs on PA 94 ascending to a woods road on Trents Hill.

SECTION 12

0.2 Turn left on woods road. A strand of laurel bushes to the right of the footpath are covered with blossoms in the springtime.

0.4 The trail turns to the left, leaving the woods road and winding through the woods. There are many sassafras trees and blueberry bushes in this section.

1.1 Turn right onto a broader trail, a portion of which may have been a woods road. Turn left and descend Trents Hill.

2.0 Reach PA 34, turn left, cross stream on highway bridge, and bear right into a field. Cross the railroad track and bear left along old rail bed.

2.8 Cross Green Mountain Road.

3.3 Cross Tagg Run. A blue-blazed trail to the left leads 0.2 mi. to the Tagg Run **SHELTERS** with a **SPRING** 500 feet beyond. Do not drink water from Tagg Run; cows pasturing upstream cause contamination.

3.4 Blue-blazed trail to the right leads to a **SPRING** near Tagg Run.

3.6 Trail bears left uphill.

4.5 Blue-blazed trail to the right leads downhill 0.7 mi. to Pine Grove Road and Mountain Creek Campground.

4.8 Cross Limekiln Road. To the left, it leads to the Village of Goodyear. To the Right, it leads 0.9 mi. downhill to Pine Grove Road.

5.9 Turn left at a junction with a blue-blazed trail which comes up from Pine Grove Road.

6.7 Old trail comes in from the left near two ant hills.

8.0 Cross Old Forge Road and begin descending Piney Mountain on a forest service road. Blue-blazed trai to the right leads 0.5 mi. to Pole Steeple. From there, a blue-blazed trail descends the cliff face and in 0.6 mi. reaches an abandoned railroad bed which is now a road in the state park.

9.2 Pass around a soapstone hole on the right.

9.4 Turn left onto the old railroad bed, now a park road, leading to Fuller Lake.

10.3 Reach a locked gate. Continuing through the park, note the ruins of the old Pine Grove Furnace on your right.

10.6 Reach PA 233, then turn left for 200 yards. Just before reaching PA 233, a grocery store is located 50 yards to your right in an old white building.

10.9 Cross PA 233 onto a stone road.

Section 12

PINE GROVE FURNACE TO PA 94

SOUTH TO NORTH

Miles   Detailed Trail Data

0.0 At the intersection of a gravel road with PA 233 turn left along the highway for 200 yards and then bear right onto Bendersville Road.

0.2 Cross a paved road and then bear left on a park road. A grocery store is 50 yards to your left on the paved road in an old white building. The Trail continues ahead through the picnic grounds. Note the ruins of the old Pine Grove Furnace on the left.

0.6 Continue past a locked gate on an old railroad bed, now a park road, passing Fuller Lake on the right.

1.5 Turn right ascending an old mountain road known as Petersburg Road.

- 1.7 Pass through an open area.

- 2.9 Reach the top of Piney Mountain and cross Old Forge Road. A blue-blazed trail to the left leads 0.5 mi. to Pole Steeple, and then descends the cliff face and in 0.6 mi. reaches an abandoned railroad bed, now a park road.

- 3.2 Turn left into the woods.

- 4.2 Continue straight ahead past old trail coming in from the right near two ant hills.

- 5.2 Turn right uphill where a blue-blazed trail comes in from the left.

- 6.3 Cross Limekiln Road. To the right it leads to the Village of Goodyear. To the left it leads downhill 0.19 mi. to Pine Grove Road.

- 6.6 Blue-blazed trail to the left leads downhill 0.7 mi. to Pine Grove Road and Mountain Creek Campground.

- 7.4 Trail turns right.

- 7.6 Blue-blazed trail to the left leads downhill to a **SPRING** near Tagg Run.

- 7.7 Blue-blazed trail to the right leads 0.2 mi. to the Tagg Run **SHELTERS** with a **SPRING** 500 feet beyond. A.T. continues ahead, crossing Tagg Run. Do not drink water from Tagg Run; cows pasturing upstream cause contamination.

- 8.1 Cross Green Mountain Road. Turn right onto old rail bed.

- 9.0 Turn right, crossing tracks and crossing old field.

- 9.1 Reach PA 34. A.T. turns left, crosses stream on highway bridge, and turns right.

- 9.2 Begin ascent of Trents Hill.

- 9.8 Bear left onto a footpath which winds through areas thick with sassafras trees and blueberry bushes.

10.5 Turn right onto a woods road where laurel blooms to the left of the trail in the springtime.

10.7 Turn right descending to PA 94.

10.9 Reach PA 94.

> To the left, in 2.5 mi. is the Village of Mount Holly Spring. A.T. continues across highway and into the woods.

Section 13

PINE GROVE FURNACE TO CALEDONIA

DISTANCE   19.7 Miles

This section of the Trail is maintained by individual overseers of the Potomac Appalachian Trail Club.

GENERAL INFORMATION

Road Approaches

At some highways the A.T. is marked by an official signboard erected by the Pennsylvania Department of Transportation or the Pennsylvania Bureau of Forestry.

Road approaches to the Trail are as follows:

0.0 mi. in Pine Grove Furnace State Park, there is adequate parking. Contact the Park Office for regulations governing the extended parking of vehicles.

2.0 mi. from Pine Grove Furnace State Park, the Trail crosses High Mountain Road, also called Michaux Road, at the site of the former Camp Michaux. Limited parking. No protection from vandalism.

8.4 mi. from Pine Grove Furnace State Park, the Trail crosses the Arendtsville-Shippensburg Road. Limited Parking. Do not park on private property without permission.

19.7 mi. from Pine Grove Furnace State Park, in Caledonia State Park, there is adequate parking. Contact the Park Office for location and for regulations governing the extended parking of vehicles.

Special Note: The Trail crosses many unimproved roads in this section, most of which are maintenance roads of the Michaux State Forest. Limited parking is possible at many of these crossings, but vandalism is an occassional problem.

Maps

KTA's map "Section 13" has been designed for use with this trail section. Map 2 and 3 (combined), "Michaux State Forest, Pennsylvania," published by the Potomac Appalachian Trail Club, also covers this section of the trail.

Shelters

3.4 mi. from Pine Grove Furnace State Park are the twin Toms Run Shelters for four persons each.

6.5 mi. from Pine Grove Furnace State Park is the Anna Michener Memorial Cabin of the PATC. This is a locked cabin with the capacity of 14 persons. Reservations to rent must be obtained in advance from the Potomac Appalachian Trail Club, 1718 N St., NW, Washington, DC 20036; telephone (202) 638-5306, weekday evenings.

9.6 mi. from Pine Grove Furnace State Park are the twin Birch Run Shelters for four persons each.

12.1 mi. from Pine Grove Furnace State Park is the Milesburn Cabin of the PATC. This is a locked cabin with a capacity of 12 persons. Reservations to rent must be obtained in advance from PATC.

17.1 mi. from Pine Grove Furnace State Park are the twin Quarry Gap Shelters for four persons each.

Public Accommodations

There is a seasonal snack bar at Fuller Lake in Pine Grove Furnace State Park and a seasonal snack bar at the swimming pool in Caledonia State Park. East of Caledonia State Park, along US 30, is a restaurant within a mile; and in 2.1 miles, Colonel's Creek Campground where cabins can be rented. To the west on US 30, 2.5 miles, is the Rite Spot Motel and Michael's Restaurant. The Ironmasters Mansion Hostel (AYH) is open year round in Pine Grove Furnace State Park.

Supplies

There is a small seasonal store in Pine Grove Furnace State Park, just off the trail near the Park headquarters. There are two grocery stores 0.9 miles west of the trail along US 30.

General Description of the Trail

Leaving Pine Grove Furnace State Park, the first six miles is a gradual ascent to the plateau-like top of South Mountain, then along the plateau with minor changes in elevation to a rather steep descent to Caledonia State Park. Points of interest along the Trail are preserved ruins of the old iron furnace in Pine Grove Furnace State Park and the small but interesting museum depicting the natural and industrial history of the area. See the Chapter on History. Going south, the Trail passes the site of the former Pine Grove Furnace Cabin of the PATC, once a farmhouse. One passes many circular flat charcoal burning hearths, 30 to 50 feet in diameter.

In the former Camp Michaux property, the trail passes the one remaining wall of a huge stone barn dating from the early days. For several years Keystone Trails Association held its fall meeting at this church camp. In World War II it had been a prisoner-of-war camp for captured German submarine personnel, and before that a CCC Camp. The Trail Shelters and the Milesburn Cabin were built by the CCC about 1935.

Big Flat Fire Tower, off the trail near the Arendtsville-Shippensburg Road, has fine views from the top and is well north the extra time.

A model iron furnace and the Thaddeus Stevens Museum are along US 30 in Caladonia State Park, 0.6 miles east of the trail.

Section 13

PINE GROVE FURNACE TO CALEDONIA

NORTH TO SOUTH

Miles   Detailed Trail Data

0.0   The Trail leaves PA 233 about 500 yards west of the park headquarters on a gravel road to the north.

0.1   Where the gravel road ends, turn left onto an old woods road.

0.7   Leaving the woods road pass several charcoal flats.

SECTION 13

1.2 Blue-blazed Sunset Rocks Trail leads to the left. For detailed trail data see the end of this section.

1.3 After crossing Toms Run on a foot bridge turn left onto the Old Shippensburg Road. To your right, uphill, was the Pine Grove Furnace Cabin of the PATC. In back of the Cabin site, the blue-blazed Wildcat Rocks Trail leads to Ridge Road and Wildcat Rocks in 2.1 miles.

1.5 Short trail to the left leads to Halfway **SPRING.**

2.0 Reach a clearing, the site of the former Camp Michaux, and the ruins of a large stone barn. A.T. turns right onto High Mountain Road, also called Michaux Road.

2.3 Trail turns left onto an abandoned road.

3.4 Reach the twin Toms Run **SHELTERS** for four persons each. **SPRING** at the rear. After crossing Toms Run the blue-blazed Sunset Rocks Trail comes in from the left. A.T. now ascends the steep slope of Antmire Hill.

4.5 Cross Woodrow Road, a forestry road passable by auto.

5.0 At the boundary of the private Tumbling Run Game Preserve turn right, paralleling Ridge Road which is a short distance to the right. (**Caution:** Do not follow the Michaux Forest boundary markers, which are also white paint.) **No camping or fires in the preserve.**

5.8 Cross the entrance road to the Preserve.

6.5 Blue-blazed trail to the left leads to the locked Anna Michener Memorial Cabin of the PATC. (See "Shelters" in General Information).

7.3 After reaching the crest of the hill, the Trail turns left crossing the old bed of Dead Woman Hollow Road, now a winter snowmobile trail.

8.4 Cross the Arendtsville-Shippensburg Road. (The trail in this area is scheduled for relocation in 1989.) A worthwhile side trip to climb the Big Flat Tower is in order.

9.6 Cross Birch Run and arrive at the twin Birch Run **SHELTERS** for 4 persons each. **SPRING** is to your right.

SECTION 13

- **10.3** Cross the old bed of Fegley Hollow Road and under a powerline.

- **10.8** Cross Michaux Forest's Rocky Knob Trail, a loop nature trail to the left. Ridge Road is a short distance to the right.

- **11.8** Cross Ridge Road and descend steeply.

- **12.1** Cross Milesburn Road. Ahead is the locked Milesburn Cabin of the PATC. (See Shelters in General Information). A blue-blazed trail to the right leads downstream and across Milesburn road to a **SPRING.** From the Milesburn Cabin climb steeply.

- **12.5** Cross the intersection of Canada Hollow Road, Means Hollow Road, and Ridge Road. The blue-blazed Rhododendron Trail goes right on Means Hollow Road in a 1.8 mile loop returning to the A.T.

- **12.9** The blue-blazed Rhododendron Trail comes in from the right. (The Rhododentron Trail is reached from Ridge Road by the Dug Hill Trail.)

- **13.0** Cross Middle Ridge Road. The A.T. now parallels Ridge Road for the next 1.4 miles.

- **14.4** Cross a TV Cable line.

- **14.8** Cross a power line cut.

- **15.6** Reach the junction of Ridge Road and Stillhouse Road which is known as Sandy Sod. At Sandy Sod the A.T. goes ahead on Ridge Road for 0.1 miles then turns left into the woods and descends through Quarry Gap.

- **16.4** Hosack Run Trail takes off to the left joining the Locust Gap Trail in 1.1 miles.

- **16.9** A.T. turns left where a stream comes in from the right and continues downhill along the stream.

- **17.1** Arrive at the twin Quarry Gap **SHELTERS** for four persons each.

- **17.4** Pass a **SPRING** on the right and the site of the former Locked Antlers Camp on the left. The A.T. is gated here to control access to the Quarry Gap **SHELTERS.**

SECTION 13

17.5 A.T. turns sharp right leaving the Quarry Gap Road.

17.7 Blue-blazed Locust Gap Trail comes in from the left on Greenwood Road. To your left, it leads 1.8 miles to the Milesburn Road and to your right 3.0 miles to Houser Road and to Fayetteville near US 30. The A.T. takes the left fork at the site of a former rifle range, then steeply descends Chinquapin Hill.

17.9 Where the Locust Gap Trail continues ahead, the A.T. turns left, passing the blue-blazed Caledonia Park Three Valley Trail. Pass two parking lots, with year-round rest rooms adjoining the second one. The road goes to the park office.

19.3 Cross Conococheague Creek on Caledonia Park bridge. **Begin 1988 relocation.** A.T. now bears to the right. The former A.T. went to the left, passing the park swimming pool and museum, to US 30. The Raccoon Run Shelters south of US 30 are to be replaced. The former A.T. is described in Section 14.

19.6 Cross bridge over former canal.

19.7 Reach US 30. PA 233 and Caledonia Park parking lot are 0.6 mi. to the east. The Michaux District Forest office is an additional 0.4 miles to the east.

DETAILED TRAIL DATA

SUNSET ROCKS TRAIL

PINE GROVE FURNACE CABIN SITE TO TOMS RUN SHELTERS

Miles   Detailed Trail Data

0.0 Where the A.T. crosses Toms Run, the blue-blazed Sunset Rocks Trail keeps to the left of the run following a woods road and acscending.

0.2 Road becomes a trail ascending more steeply.

0.4 Reach the crest of the ridge, turn right (to the left, a short spur trail provides good views) and follow through and up over boulders. Use care!

1.1 Turn right onto High Mountain (Michaux) Road.

1.4 Turn left onto an old woods road, then follow the wire fence of the former Camp Michaux.

2.4 Reach the A.T., at 3.4 miles from PA 233 in Pine Grove Furnace Park, just 30 yards beyond its crossing of Toms Run. Shelters are another 30 yards to the right.

DETAILED TRAIL DATA

SUNSET ROCKS TRAIL

TOMS RUN SHELTERS TO PINE GROVE FURNACE CABIN SITE

Miles   Detailed Trail Data

0.0 30 yards before reaching Toms Run and 60 yards before the shelters, this blue-blazed trail leads right, then along a wire fence of the former Camp Michaux for 0.5 mile.

1.0 Turn right onto High Mountain (Michaux) Road.

1.3 Turn left onto a woods road ascending Little Rocky Ridge.

1.9 Reach the crest of Sunset Rocks and follow through up and over boulders. Use care!

2.0 Turn left from the ridge crest and descend. A short spur trail goes straight ahead, providing good views.

2.4 Reach the A.T. To the left, across Toms Run, is the site of the former Pine Grove Furnace Cabin of the PATC.

Section 13

CALEDONIA TO PINE GROVE FURNACE

SOUTH TO NORTH

Miles   Detailed Trail Data

0.0 Cross US Highway 30. To the east 0.6 miles is PA Highway 233 with Caledonia Park parking lots, and Michaux District Forester's office an additional 0.4 miles.

SECTION 13

0.1 Cross bridge over former canal.

0.4 Reach bridge over Conococheague Creek in Caledonia State Park. Former A.T. comes in from the right. Pass two parking lots with year-round rest rooms beside the first one. Climb steeply between Orebank Hill on the left and Chinquapin Hill on the right.

1.8 The Caledonia Park Three Valley Trail comes in from the left.

2.0 Reach the site of a former rifle range. Blue-blazed Locust Gap Trail comes in on the left 3.0 miles from the Fayetville area on Greenwood Road near US 30 and leads 1.8 miles to the right to Milesburn Road.

2.2 Pass the site of the former Locked Antlers Camp and **SPRING** on the right. The A.T. is gated here to control access to the Quarry Gap Shelters.

2.6 Arrive Quarry Gap twin **SHELTERS** for four persons each.

3.3 Hosack Run Trail takes off to the right joining the Locust Gap Trail in 1.1 miles.

4.0 Reach the top of the hill and turn right onto Ridge Road.

4.1 At Sandy Sod, the junction of Stillhouse Road and Ridge Road, cross the intersection and turn left off Ridge Road into the woods.

6.7 Cross Middle Ridge Road. In the next half-mile is a view of the Big Flat Fire Tower 4.8 miles ahead by Trail.

6.8 Blue-blazed Rhododendron Trail comes in from left. Michaux Forest's Dug Hill Trail goes right to Ridge Road.

7.2 Cross the intersection of Canada Hollow Road, Means Hollow Road, and Ridge Road. Blue-blazed Rhododendron Trail, a 1.8-mile loop, comes in from the left on Means Hollow Road.

7.6 Reach the locked Milesburn Cabin of the PATC. Reservations to rent must be obtained in advance from PATC. A blue-blazed trail to the left leads down stream and across Milesburn Road to a **SPRING**. A.T. crosses Milesburn Road and ascends steeply.

SECTION 13

7.9 Cross Ridge Road. Pass under power line.

8.9 Cross Michaux Forest's Rocky Knob Trail. Ridge Road is a short distance to the left.

9.4 Cross under a power line and then cross the bed of former Fegley Road.

10.1 Arrive Birch Run twin **SHELTERS** on the right for four persons each. **SPRING** on your left. Trail continues ahead, crossing Birch Run.

11.3 Cross the Arendtsville-Shipensburg Road. A worthwhile side trip to climb the Big Flat Fire Tower is in order. To reach the tower, turn left onto the Arendtsville-Shippensburg Road and then turn right onto Ridge Road. In a short distance beyond the radio tower you will see the tower on your left. Fine views from the top.

12.4 Cross the bed of the former Dead Woman Hollow Road, now a wintertime snowmobile trail. A long descent is ahead with views of Mount Holly and Long Mountain in the distance.

13.2 Blue-blazed trail to the right leads 0.2 mile to the locked Anna Michener Memorial Cabin of the PATC. Reservations to rent must be obtained from the PATC in advance.

13.9 Cross the entrance road to the private Tumbling Run Game Preserve. **No camping or fires in the Preserve.** Trail turns right, then left, generally following the boundary of the game preserve.

15.2 Cross Woodrow Road with fine outlooks.

16.2 Blue-blazed Sunset Rocks Trail goes off to the right. For details of this trail, see the end of the North to South trail description for this section.

16.3 Arrive at the twin Toms Run **SHELTERS** for four persons each. **SPRING** in back of shelters.

17.4 Turn right onto High Mountain Road, also called Michaux Road, then passing into the side of the former Camp Michaux.

17.6 Trail turns left passing the ruins of an old stone barn.

SECTION 13

18.1 A.T. bears right where the road forks. Side trail to the right leads 50 yards to Half Way **SPRING.**

18.4 Pass the site of the former Pine Grove Furnace Cabin of the PATC on your left. In back of the cabin site, the blue-blazed Wildcat Rocks Trail leads to the Ridge Road and Wildcat Rocks in 2.1 miles. Across the foot bridge the blue-blazed Sunset Rocks Trail leads uphill to the right. See details at the end of the North to South trail description for this section. A.T. bears right crossing Toms Run on a foot bridge.

18.6 Cross a small brook, then pass old charcoal flats which provided fuel for Pine Grove Furnace in the 1700's. Trail bears right, then left.

19.0 Trail follows an old woods road.

19.6 Turn right onto a gravel road.

19.7 Reach PA 233 and turn left for about 200 yards, then turn right onto Bendersville Road entering Pine Grove Furnace State Park. The first road to the left passes the seasonally operated park store, an old white building, in 50 yards, and continues on to the park headquarters building which is located on PA 233.

Section 14

CALEDONIA TO PEN MAR

DISTANCE 17.1 Miles

This section of the Trail is maintained by individual overseers of the Potomac Appalachian Trail Club.

GENERAL INFORMATION

Road Approaches

At some highways the A.T. is marked by an official signboard erected by the Pennsylvania Department of Transportation or the Pennsylvania Bureau of Forestry.

Road approaches to the Trail are as follows:

0.0 mi. on US Highway 30, at approximately the mid-point between Gettysburg and Chambersburg, the Trail crosses US 30 0.6 mi. west of the intersection with PA 233. Adequate parking nearby. Contact the park office for regulations governing the extended parking of vehicles.

4.6 mi. from Caledonia State Park the Trail crosses PA 233. Limited parking. No protection from vandals.

9.4 mi. from Caledonia State Park the Trail crosses Antietam Road near the Old Forge Picnic Ground. Limited parking.

10.1 mi. from Caledonia State Park the Trail reaches the edge of the playing field of Old Forge Picnic Grounds. Limited parking.

14.6 mi. from Caledonia State Park the Trail crosses PA 16 between Rouzerville and Blue Ridge Summit. Limited parking.

17.1 mi. from Caledonia State Park the Trail goes through the village of Pen Mar. Limited parking. Do not trespass. Parking is available in Pen Mar County Park in Maryland.

SECTION 14
Maps

KTA's map "Section 14" has been designed for use with this trail section. Map #4, "Mont Alto Section" published by the Potomac Appalachian Trail Club, also covers this section of the trail.

Shelters

1.8 mi. from Caledonia State Park, **on the former A.T. route,** are the twin Raccoon Run Shelters for 4 persons each. These shelters are scheduled for eventual relocation.

8.1 mi. from Caledonia State Park is the locked Hermitage Cabin of the PATC, located .9 mi. off the Trail. Reservations to rent must be obtained in advance from the Potomac Appalachian Trail Club, 1718 N. St., N.W., Washington, D.C. 20036.

9.3 mi. from Caledonia State Park on a blue-blazed side trail is the Tumbling Run Shelter for 6 persons.

10.2 mi. from Caledonia State Park is the Antietam Shelter for 6 persons, just beyond the Old Forge Picnic Grounds.

14.4 mi. from Caledonia State Park is the Mackie Run Shelter for 6 persons, scheduled for relocation.

Public Accommodations

There is a seasonal snack bar at the swimming pool in Caledonia State Park. East of Caledonia State Park, along US 30, is a restaurant within a mile. To the east 2.1 miles, Colonel's Creek Campground rents cabins. To the west on US 30, 2.5 mi., is Rite Spot Motel and Restaurant. On PA 16, about 0.6 mi. east of the Trail, are the Mountain Top Pines Cabins. There are several restaurants in Blue Ridge Summit, 1.8 mi. east of the Trail on PA 16.

Supplies

There are 2 grocery stores 0.9 miles west of Caledonia State Park along US 30. In the village of South Mountain, about 5.0 miles south of Caledonia State Park and 1.1 miles east of the Trail, along Sanatorium Road, is located Smith's Grocery and Gas, newly enlarged and remodeled, as well as a post office. Along PA 16, there are stores in Rouzerville 2.5 miles west of the Trail and in Blue Ridge Summit 1.8 miles east of the trail.

General Description of the Trail

Most of the Trail, in this section, is through pleasing woods on Rocky Mountain. The main climb to Snowy Mountain is gradual with a descent to the Old Forge Picnic Grounds area, and a steep climb up to Pen Mar. Watch out for the white paint boundary markings of the State Forest Lands, which cross the A.T. and are similar to A.T. blazes, causing some confusion. The latter are 2" x 6" and face the hiker. The others are quite irregular. Points of interest along the Trail are the Snowy Mountain Fire Tower, Chimney Rocks, the Old Forge Picnic Ground, and an original marker of the Mason-Dixon Line at Pen Mar, now on private property. The Chapter on History details the story of Pen Mar Park and the Caledonia Park area.

Section 14

CALEDONIA TO PEN MAR

NORTH TO SOUTH

Miles   **Detailed Trail Data**

NOTE: The first five miles of Section 14 is part of a stretch, beginning at mile 19.3 in Section 13, that was relocated in 1988.

0.0   Cross US 30, 0.6 mi. west of PA 233. Parking at that intersection in Caledonia State Park.

0.1   Cross gas pipe line. Begin steady uphill climb.

4.4   Cross a maintenance road.

4.6   Reach PA 233. To the left (east) 1.6 mi. is the village of South Mountain, with store and post office. PA 233 goes north to Caledonia State Park and US 30. To the right PA 233 goes to the villge of Mont Alto, Mont Alto School of Forestry of Penn State University, and Mont Alto State Park.

4.8   Former A.T. comes in on the left. (End of 1988 relocation.)

4.9	Turn left on "Swamp Road" through a very boggy area.
5.0	Turn right (south) off "Swamp Road" on an abandoned road used by firewood cutters.
5.3	Cross dirt road (closed to public)
5.6	Cross Snowy Mountain Road (end of 1981 relocation) ascending.
6.1	A.T. leads straight ahead. Blue-blazed trail to the right leads 0.1 mile to Snowy Mountain Fire Tower with fine views from the top.
6.2	Cross under a power line.
7.3	Cross a pipeline.
8.1	A.T. continues ahead descending. Blue-blazed trail to the left leads 0.1 mile to Chimney Rocks, at 1,940 feet of elevation, with a magnificent view over Green Ridge and the Waynesboro Reservoir. Blue-blazed trail to the right leads 0.9 mile down to the locked Hermitage Cabin of the PATC. Reservations to rent must be obtained in advance from PATC. (See Shelters in General Information.) Blue-blazed trail continues on and in another 0.5 mile reaches the Tumbling Run Shelter and then rejoins the A.T.
9.3	Blue-blazed trail to the right leads north to the Tumbling Run **SHELTER** and the Hermitage Cabin of PATC.
9.4	Reach paved Antietam Road, turn right across bridge, then left into woods. Antietam Road (also called Old Forge Road) straight ahead leads to the Old Forge Picnic Grounds, and then onto the Antietam **SHELTER** for 6 persons. **WATER** can be obtained in the summer at the fountains in the picnic grounds. A frost free tap on the well housing allows hikers to obtain water in the winter months. DO NOT drink water from Antietam Creek.
9.5	Bear right off old Trail (relocated in 1981).

SECTION 14

9.9 — Cross Rattlesnake Run Road. High water route on Rattlesnake Run Road to left is blue-blazed, if bridge over Little Antietam Creek is not passable.

10.1 — Reach edge of Old Forge Picnic Grounds and frost free **WATER** tap on well housing.

10.2 — Bear right on water pipe-line right-of-way, then re-enter woods. Antietam shelter (described above) is visible on left.

10.3 — Cross stream on bridge. (See Rattlesnake Run Road, above, in case of high water.) Rejoin original A.T. (end of 1981 relocation).

10.8 — Turn sharp left uphill.

11.7 — Turn right onto an abandoned woods road.

12.2 — Cross a pipeline.

12.6 — Pass a **SPRING** on the left near a burned out hunting camp. This is the site to which the Mackie Run Shelter will eventually be located.

13.7 — Reach Bailey **SPRING,** an excellent walled spring, always running. A.T. goes right from the spring for 25 yards then left uphill. Use care following blazes due to Forest boundary blazes. Fill canteens here for Mackie Run Shelter.

14.0 — Recross Rattlesnake Run Road. Reach Mentzer Gap Road. Cross Mackie Run. A blue-blazed trail leads 50 yards to the left to Mackie **SPRING, usually dry after June.** A.T. turns right off Mentzer Gap Road.

14.4 — Pass Mackie Run **SHELTER** for 6 persons just off A.T. on blue-blazed trail. Do not drink from Mackie Run, nearest dependable water is back at Bailey Spring. (This shelter is to be replaced. See mile 12.6, above.)

14.6 — Trail reaches PA 16. Rouzerville is 2.1 mi. west o the right; Blue Ridge Summit is 1.8 miles east, to the left. A.T. crosses PA 16 then crossing Red Run, then crossing a line of white blazes marking the southern boundaries of Michaux State Forest. Begin 1986 relocation.

SECTION 14

14.9	Cross old PA 16.
16.0	Cross Buena Vista Road, with roadside **SPRING** on the right. Several miles to the right is the site of the former Buena Vista Hotel.
16.5	Cross Falls Creek on trail bridge.
16.6	Turn left onto old trolley line road bed, which once served Pen Mar Park.
16.9	Turn right onto power line right-of-way.
17.0	Cross Pen Mar Road.
17.1	Enter Maryland. In 0.1 mi. cross railroad tracks and enter Washington County's PenMar Park. End of 1986 relocation.

NOTE: The Mason-Dixon marker Mile 91 from the 1765 survey is no longer accessible from the A.T.

END OF SOUTHERN DIVISION

FORMER ROUTE OF APPALACHIAN TRAIL

NOTE: The former route of the A.T., from Caledonia State Park to PA 233 near Sanatorium Road and the lilypond, has been blue-blazed. During 1988 the route is being evaluated as a potential circuit hike from the park. This route passes the park outdoor church, Raccoon Run Shelter (which will be relocated), Rocky Mountain Creek, and Corls Ridge. Trail description is as follows, from north to south, starting in Caledonia State Park.

0.0	In Section 13 of this guidebook, at mile 19.3, where the A.T. bears right after crossing the Caledonia Park bridge over Conococheague Creek, the former A.T. turns to the left (east), passing the park swimming pool and summer concession stand, recreation fields, and the Thaddeus Stevens Museum.

SECTION 14

0.3	Reach US 30. Bear left, crossing highway bridges over Carbaugh and Rocky Mountain Creeks. A model iron furnace is on the north edge of the parking area at this intersection. Turn right (south) on PA 233 and immediately left on Golf Course Road. The golf course and Totem Pole Playhouse are ahead on this road.
0.4	Trail bears right off the road to follow the stream bank, passing the outdoor church and a private cabin on the left.
0.5	Turn left away from stream and ascend steeply.
1.2	Cross small stream. Cabins upstream make this an undesirable water source.
1.4	Cross stream on Perry Road culvert before a short steep ascent.
1.9	Cross Corls Road.
2.2	Reach twin Raccoon Run **SHELTERS**, which are to be relocated. A blue-blazed spur trail leads left on District Road for 70 yards to a **SPRING**. Water from Raccoon Run must be boiled. Trail crosses Raccoon Run on District Road bridge.
2.5	Cross Corls Ridge Road (closed to traffic).
4.0	Bear right. This was the beginning of the 1981 A.T. relocation off Corls Ridge Road which is ahead. This section of Corls Ridge Road is accessible by car from the south off Sanatorium Road.
4.6	Cross Rocky Mountain Creek on YCC bridge.
4.7	Cross PA 233 again. To left is Sanatorium Road and the village of South Mountain. A large lilypond is at the junction.
5.4	Reach the A.T. To the right is the 1988 relocation to Caledonia Park. Straight ahead is the southbound Trail to Swamp Road.

Section 14

PEN MAR TO CALEDONIA

SOUTH TO NORTH

Miles   **Detailed Trail Data**

NOTE: The next 2.5 miles (and the preceding 0.1 mi. in Maryland) were relocated in 1986. The Mason-Dixon marker for Mile 91 is on private property and no longer accessible from the A.T.

0.0   In Pen Mar Park, bear left just before reaching Pen Mar Road. Cross railroad tracks and enter Pennsylvania.

0.1   Turn right on power line right-of-way and cross Pen Mar Road, continuing on right-of-way.

0.2   Turn left off right-of-way.

0.4   Turn left on old trolley line road bed which once served Pen Mar Park.

0.5   Cross Falls Creek on trail bridge. Bear right uphill after crossing second span.

1.1   Cross Buena Vista Road. There is a roadside **SPRING** to the left. Several miles to the left is the site of the former Buena Vista Hotel.

2.2   Cross old PA Route 16.

2.5   Cross PA Route 16. (End of 1986 relocation). Rouzerville is 2.4 miles west, to the left; Blue Ridge Summit is 1.8 miles east, to the right.

2.7   Reach Mackie Run **SHELTER** for 6 persons, on a blue-blazed trail to the left. (This shelter is to be replaced). Do not drink from Mackie Run. A.T. continues on crossing Mentzer Gap Road. A blue-blazed trail to the right leads 50 yards to Mackie **SPRING, usually dry after June.** Nearest dependable water is at Bailey Spring 0.7 mile ahead.

SECTION 14

2.8	Cross Mackie Run on Metzer Gap Road.
3.1	Cross Rattlesnake Run Road.
3.4	Reach Bailey **SPRING**, an excellent walled spring. Always running.
4.5	Pass a **SPRING** on the right near a burned out hunting camp. This is the site where the Mackie Run Shelter replacement will eventually be located.
4.9	Cross a pipeline.
5.4	Cross woods road.
6.3	Turn right descending gradually.
6.8	Approach Little Antietam Creek. High water route (blue-blazed) turns right upstream and in 0.2 mile reaches Rattlesnake Run Road. Trail crosses creek on bridge. Antietam **SHELTER** is on right, for 6 persons. Do not drink water from the creek. If the creek is too high to cross, take the high water route via Rattlesnake Run Road and follow the A.T. southbound to the shelter. **WATER** is obtainable in the summer months from the fountains at the picnic grounds. There is a frost free tap on well housing for winter use.
7.0	Reach frost free tap on well housing at edge of Old Forge Picnic Grounds.
7.2	Cross Rattlesnake Run Road. Blue-blazed high water route described above comes in on right.
7.6	Rejoin original A.T. coming in on right, (relocated in 1981).
7.7	Cross Tumbling Run on Antietam Road (sometimes called Old Forge Road) bridge.
7.8	A.T. turns right and begins ascending gradually, then steeply. Blue-blazed trail, ahead, leads to Tumbling Run **SHELTER** in 100 yards and then to Hermitage Cabin of the PATC, a locked cabin for 12 in 0.5 miles. Reservations to rent must be obtained in advance from PATC. (See Shelters in General Information).

SECTION 14

9.0	Blue-blazed trail to the right leads 0.1 mile to Chimney Rocks, at 1,940 feet of elevation, with a magnificent outlook over Green Ridge and Waynesboro Reservoir. Blue-blazed trail to the left leads 0.9 mile down to the Hermitage Cabin of the PATC. A.T. continues ahead.
9.8	Cross a pipeline.
10.9	Cross under a power line.
11.0	Blue-blazed side trail to left leads 0.1 mile to Snowy Mountain Fire Tower with fine views from the top.
11.5	Cross Snowy Mountain Road. Begin 1981 relocation off several roads.
11.8	Cross dirt road (closed to public).
12.1	Reach "Swamp Road". Turn left on road across very boggy area.
12.2	Turn right off "Swamp Road."
12.3	Turn left. Former A.T. comes in from straight ahead. Begin 1988 relocation.
12.5	Cross PA 233. To the right (east) 1.6 mi. is the village of South Mountain with store and Post Office. PA 233 goes north to Caledonia Park and US 30. To the left, PA 233 goes to the village of Mont Alto, Mont Alto School of Forestry of Penn State University, and Mont Alto State Park.
12.7	Cross a maintenance road.
17.0	Cross gas pipe line.
17.1	Reach US 30. To the right (east) is PA 233 and Caledonia State Park parking lot. Michaux District Forester's office is 0.4 miles beyond. To the left (west) 0.9 mi. are two stores, and a motel and restaurant are an additional 1.6 mi. The 1988 relocation ends 0.4 mi. ahead in Caledonia State Park, described in Section 13.

INDEX

TOPIC	PAGE
Abbreviations	2
Allentown Shelter	62, 63, 71
Antietam Shelter	140, 142, 147
Avery, Myron H.	6
Bailey Spring	143, 147
Bake Oven Knob	58, 59
Bake Oven Knob Shelter	56, 58, 59
Ballard, Edward B.	6
Bashore Boy Scout Reservation	87, 88
Birch Run Shelters	130, 132, 137
Blazing	28
Blue Mountain Camp (YWCA)	62, 66, 68
Blue Mountain Summit	58, 59, 63, 71
Blue Rocks	65, 69
Caledonia Iron Works	14
Caledonia State Park	23, 134, 135, 136, 140
Campbell Spring Shelter	117, 119, 121
Center Point Knob	119, 121
Chimney Rocks	142, 148
Clarks Ferry Bridge	95, 99, 103, 104, 105, 109
Clarks Ferry Shelter	96, 98, 100
Dan's Pulpit	64, 70
Darlington Shelter	104, 106, 107
Darlington Trail	104, 106, 107
Duncannon	102, 104, 108
Eagle Nest Shelter	73, 76, 77
Fumitory Rocks	97, 101
Game Commission Camping Rules	21
Hawk Mountain Sanctuary	19-20, 64, 65, 70
Hawk Rock	104, 108
Hermitage Cabin	140, 147, 148
Hertlein Campsite	81, 84
Horse-Shoe Trail	89, 90, 92
Katellen Trail	51, 54
Kimmel, Richard	81, 84
Kirkridge Shelter	44, 45, 47
Locust Gap Trail	134, 136
MacKaye, Benton	5
Mackie Run Shelter	140, 143, 146
Map, Pa. Highway	1
Metric Conversion Table	3

TOPIC	PAGE
Michaux State Forest	129, 137
Michaux, Camp	129, 131, 132, 135, 137
Michener, Anna Memorial Cabin	130, 132, 137
Milesburn Cabin	130, 133, 136
Mt. Alto Iron Works	15
Musser Farm	112
New Tripoli Campsite	58, 59
Outerbridge, George W. Shelter	56, 57, 60
Pen Mar	139
Pen Mar Park	15, 144, 146
Perkins, Arthur	6
Peters Mountain Shelter	95, 97, 100
Pilger Ruh Spring	81, 84
Pine Grove Furnace	14, 126, 131, 138
Pine Grove Furnace State Park	24, 124, 129, 130, 131, 138, 139
Pinnacle	65, 69
Pocohontas Spring	66, 68
Pole Steeple	124, 125, 127
Presbyterian Church of the Mountain	44
Pulpit Rock	66, 69
Quarry Gap Shelters	130, 133, 136
Raccoon Run Shelters	134, 140, 145
Rausch Gap	88, 90, 92
Rausch Gap Shelter	88, 90, 92
Rentschler, Dr. H. F.	76, 77
Rhododendron Trail	133, 136
Showers Steps	81, 84
Smith, Leroy A. Shelter	50, 51, 54
St. Anthony's Wilderness	12, 88
Stevens, Thaddeus Museum	131
Sunset Rocks Trail	132, 134-135, 137, 138
Swatara State Park	24
Tagg Run Shelters	123, 125, 127
Thelma Marks Memorial Shelter	104, 108
Toms Run Shelters	130, 132
Tri-County Corner	64, 71
Tumbling Run Shelter	140, 142, 147
Tuscarora Trail	104
Walking Purchase	10
Waterville Bridge	82, 83
Whiskey Spring	119, 121
White Rocks Ridge	118, 119, 121

TOPIC	PAGE
Windsor Furnace	66, 68
Windsor Furnace Shelter	62, 66, 68
Wolf Rocks	46, 47
Yeich Spring	73, 76, 77
Yellow Springs Village	88, 90, 91
Zeager Shelter	96, 97, 100